Connected Mathematics

Ruins of Montarek

Spatial Visualization

Teacher's Edition

Glenda Lappan
James T. Fey
William M. Fitzgerald
Susan N. Friel
Elizabeth Difanis Phillips

Developed at Michigan State University

DALE SEYMOUR PUBLICATIONS®
MENLO PARK, CALIFORNIA

Connected Mathematics™ was developed at Michigan State University with financial support from the Michigan State University Office of the Provost, Computing and Technology, and the College of Natural Science.

This material is based upon work supported by the National Science Foundation under Grant No. MDR 9150217.

This project was supported, in part,
by the
National Science Foundation
Opinions expressed are those of the authors
and not necessarily those of the Foundation

The Michigan State University authors and administration have agreed that all MSU royalties arising from this publication will be devoted to purposes supported by the Department of Mathematics and the MSU Mathematics Education Enrichment Fund.

This book is published by Dale Seymour Publications®, an imprint of Addison Wesley Longman, Inc.

Dale Seymour Publications
2725 Sand Hill Road
Menlo Park, CA 94025
Customer Service: 800 872-1100

Managing Editor: Catherine Anderson
Project Editor: Stacey Miceli
Book Editor: Mali Apple
Revision Editor: James P. McAuliffe
ESL Consultant: Nancy Sokol Green
Production/Manufacturing Director: Janet Yearian
Production/Manufacturing Coordinators: Claire Flaherty, Alan Noyes
Design Manager: John F. Kelly
Photo Editor: Roberta Spieckerman
Design: Don Taka
Composition: London Road Design, Palo Alto, CA
Electronic Prepress Revision: A. W. Kingston Publishing Services, Chandler, AZ
Illustrations: Pauline Phung, Margaret Copeland, Ray Godfrey
Cover: Ray Godfrey

Photo Acknowledgements: 7 (architect) © Spencer Grant/FPG International; 7 (construction) © Norman R. Rowan/Stock, Boston; 10 © Gene Ahrens/FPG International; 13 © George Holton/Photo Researchers, Inc.; 26 © Arvind Garg/Photo Researchers, Inc.; 35 © Roy Bishop/Stock, Boston; 52 © T. Holton/Superstock, Inc.; 67 © Sam C. Pierson, Jr./Photo Researchers, Inc.; 68 © S. Vidler/Superstock, Inc.; 79 © C. Orrico/Superstock, Inc.

**DALE
SEYMOUR
PUBLICATIONS®**

Order number 45818
ISBN 1-57232-623-9

1 2 3 4 5 6 7 8 9 10-ML-01 00 99 98 97

The Connected Mathematics Project Staff

Project Directors

James T. Fey
University of Maryland

William M. Fitzgerald
Michigan State University

Susan N. Friel
University of North Carolina at Chapel Hill

Glenda Lappan
Michigan State University

Elizabeth Difanis Phillips
Michigan State University

Project Manager

Kathy Burgis
Michigan State University

Technical Coordinator

Judith Martus Miller
Michigan State University

Collaborating Teachers/Writers

Mary K. Bouck
Portland, Michigan

Jacqueline Stewart
Okemos, Michigan

Curriculum Development Consultants

David Ben-Chaim
Weizmann Institute

Alex Friedlander
Weizmann Institute

Eleanor Geiger
University of Maryland

Jane Mitchell
University of North Carolina at Chapel Hill

Anthony D. Rickard
Alma College

Evaluation Team

Mark Hoover
Michigan State University

Diane V. Lambdin
Indiana University

Sandra K. Wilcox
Michigan State University

Judith S. Zawojewski
National-Louis University

Graduate Assistants

Scott J. Baldridge
Michigan State University

Angie S. Eshelman
Michigan State University

M. Faaiz Gierdien
Michigan State University

Jane M. Keiser
Indiana University

Angela S. Krebs
Michigan State University

James M. Larson
Michigan State University

Ronald Preston
Indiana University

Tat Ming Sze
Michigan State University

Sarah Theule-Lubienski
Michigan State University

Jeffrey J. Wanko
Michigan State University

Field Test Production Team

Katherine Oesterle
Michigan State University

Stacey L. Otto
University of North Carolina at Chapel Hill

Teacher/Assessment Team

Kathy Booth
Waverly, Michigan

Anita Clark
Marshall, Michigan

Theodore Gardella
Bloomfield Hills, Michigan

Yvonne Grant
Portland, Michigan

Linda R. Lobue
Vista, California

Suzanne McGrath
Chula Vista, California

Nancy McIntyre
Troy, Michigan

Linda Walker
Tallahassee, Florida

Software Developer

Richard Burgis
East Lansing, Michigan

Development Center Directors

Nicholas Branca
San Diego State University

Dianne Briars
Pittsburgh Public Schools

Frances R. Curcio
New York University

Perry Lanier
Michigan State University

J. Michael Shaughnessy
Portland State University

Charles Vonder Embse
Central Michigan University

Field Test Coordinators

Michelle Bohan
Queens, New York

Melanie Branca
San Diego, California

Alecia Devantier
Shepherd, Michigan

Jenny Jorgensen
Flint, Michigan

Sandra Kralovec
Portland, Oregon

Sonia Marsalis
Flint, Michigan

William Schaeffer
Pittsburgh, Pennsylvania

Karma Vince
Toledo, Ohio

Virginia Wolf
Pittsburgh, Pennsylvania

Shirel Yaloz
Queens, New York

Student Assistants

Laura Hammond
David Roche
Courtney Stoner
Jovan Trpovski
Julie Valicenti
Michigan State University

Patricia Wagner
Holmes Middle School

Greg Williams
Gundry Elementary School

Lansing

Susan Bissonette
Waverly Middle School

Kathy Booth
Waverly East Intermediate School

Carole Campbell
Waverly East Intermediate School

Gary Gillespie
Waverly East Intermediate School

Denise Kehren
Waverly Middle School

Virginia Larson
Waverly East Intermediate School

Kelly Martin
Waverly Middle School

Laurie Metevier
Waverly East Intermediate School

Craig Paksi
Waverly East Intermediate School

Tony Pecoraro
Waverly Middle School

Helene Rewa
Waverly East Intermediate School

Arnold Stiefel
Waverly Middle School

Portland

Bill Carlton
Portland Middle School

Kathy Dole
Portland Middle School

Debby Flate
Portland Middle School

Yvonne Grant
Portland Middle School

Terry Keusch
Portland Middle School

John Manzini
Portland Middle School

Mary Parker
Portland Middle School

Scott Sandborn
Portland Middle School

Shepherd

Steve Brant
Shepherd Middle School

Marty Brock
Shepherd Middle School

Cathy Church
Shepherd Middle School

Ginny Crandall
Shepherd Middle School

Craig Ericksen
Shepherd Middle School

Natalie Hackney
Shepherd Middle School

Bill Hamilton
Shepherd Middle School

Julie Salisbury
Shepherd Middle School

Sturgis

Sandra Allen
Eastwood Elementary School

Margaret Baker
Eastwood Elementary School

Steven Baker
Eastwood Elementary School

Keith Barnes
Sturgis Middle School

Wilodean Beckwith
Eastwood Elementary School

Darcy Bird
Eastwood Elementary School

Bill Dickey
Sturgis Middle School

Ellen Eisele
Sturgis Middle School

James Hoelscher
Sturgis Middle School

Richard Nolan
Sturgis Middle School

J. Hunter Raiford
Sturgis Middle School

Cindy Sprowl
Eastwood Elementary School

Leslie Stewart
Eastwood Elementary School

Connie Sutton
Eastwood Elementary School

Traverse City

Maureen Bauer
Interlochen Elementary School

Ivanka Berskshire
East Junior High School

Sarah Boehm
Courtade Elementary School

Marilyn Conklin
Interlochen Elementary School

Nancy Crandall
Blair Elementary School

Fran Cullen
Courtade Elementary School

Eric Dreier
Old Mission Elementary School

Lisa Dzierwa
Cherry Knoll Elementary School

Ray Fouch
West Junior High School

Ed Hargis
Willow Hill Elementary School

Richard Henry
West Junior High School

Dessie Hughes
Cherry Knoll Elementary School

Ruthanne Kladder
Oak Park Elementary School

Bonnie Knapp
West Junior High School

Sue Laisure
Sabin Elementary School

Stan Malaski
Oak Park Elementary School

Jody Meyers
Sabin Elementary School

Marsha Myles
East Junior High School

Mary Beth O'Neil
Traverse Heights Elementary School

Jan Palkowski
East Junior High School

Karen Richardson
Old Mission Elementary School

Kristin Sak
Bertha Vos Elementary School

Mary Beth Schmitt
East Junior High School

Mike Schrotenboer
Norris Elementary School

Gail Smith
Willow Hill Elementary School

Karrie Tufts
Eastern Elementary School

Mike Wilson
East Junior High School

Tom Wilson
West Junior High School

Minnesota

Minneapolis

Betsy Ford
Northeast Middle School

New York

East Elmhurst

Allison Clark
Louis Armstrong Middle School

Dorothy Hershey
Louis Armstrong Middle School

J. Lewis McNeece
Louis Armstrong Middle School

Rossana Perez
Louis Armstrong Middle School

Merna Porter
Louis Armstrong Middle School

Marie Turini
Louis Armstrong Middle School

North Carolina

Durham

Everly Broadway
Durham Public Schools

Thomas Carson
Duke School for Children

Mary Hebrank
Duke School for Children

Bill O'Connor
Duke School for Children

Ruth Pershing
Duke School for Children

Peter Reichert
Duke School for Children

Elizabeth City

Rita Banks
Elizabeth City Middle School

Beth Chaundry
Elizabeth City Middle School

Amy Cuthbertson
Elizabeth City Middle School

Deni Dennison
Elizabeth City Middle School

Jean Gray
Elizabeth City Middle School

John McMenamin
Elizabeth City Middle School

Nicollette Nixon
Elizabeth City Middle School

Malinda Norfleet
Elizabeth City Middle School

Joyce O'Neal
Elizabeth City Middle School

Clevie Sawyer
Elizabeth City Middle School

Juanita Shannon
Elizabeth City Middle School

Terry Thorne
Elizabeth City Middle School

Rebecca Wardour
Elizabeth City Middle School

Leora Winslow
Elizabeth City Middle School

Franklinton

Susan Haywood
Franklinton Elementary School

Clyde Melton
Franklinton Elementary School

Louisburg

Lisa Anderson
Terrell Lane Middle School

Jackie Frazier
Terrell Lane Middle School

Pam Harris
Terrell Lane Middle School

Ohio

Toledo

Bonnie Bias
Hawkins Elementary School

Marsha Jackish
Hawkins Elementary School

Lee Jagodzinski
DeVeaux Junior High School

Norma J. King
Old Orchard Elementary School

Margaret McCready
Old Orchard Elementary School

Carmella Morton
DeVeaux Junior High School

Karen C. Rohrs
Hawkins Elementary School

Marie Sahloff
DeVeaux Junior High School

L. Michael Vince
McTigue Junior High School

Brenda D. Watkins
Old Orchard Elementary School

Oregon

Portland

Roberta Cohen
Catlin Gabel School

David Ellenberg
Catlin Gabel School

Sara Normington
Catlin Gabel School

Karen Scholte-Arce
Catlin Gabel School

West Linn

Marge Burack
Wood Middle School

Tracy Wygant
Athey Creek Middle School

Canby

Sandra Kralovec
Ackerman Middle School

Pennsylvania

Pittsburgh

Sheryl Adams
Reizenstein Middle School

Sue Barie
Frick International Studies Academy

Suzie Berry
Frick International Studies Academy

Richard Delgrosso
Frick International Studies Academy

Janet Falkowski
Frick International Studies Academy

Joanne George
Reizenstein Middle School

Harriet Hopper
Reizenstein Middle School

Chuck Jessen
Reizenstein Middle School

Ken Labuskes
Reizenstein Middle School

Barbara Lewis
Reizenstein Middle School

Sharon Mihalich
Reizenstein Middle School

Marianne O'Connor
Frick International Studies Academy

Mark Sammartino
Reizenstein Middle School

Washington

Seattle

Chris Johnson
University Preparatory Academy

Rick Purn
University Preparatory Academy

Contents

Mathematics textbooks, even at the elementary level, are filled with pictures depicting solid objects. These images will likely make immediate sense to adults. Children, however—especially children who have had little opportunity to create and examine models of solid objects—may find such drawings extremely confusing.

Research shows that when middle-school students are presented with a drawing such as the one shown here and a simple question such as, "How many cubes does it take to build this solid?" they often misinterpret what the back of the solid looks like.

Many students will count every *face* of every cube showing and report the total as the answer; they are aware only of the figure's two-dimensional aspects. Others will offer twice this total as the answer; they are aware of the hidden part of the drawing, but have an incorrect image of the relationship between the picture and the cubes in the actual solid. Some will count each *cube* showing and give twice this number as the answer; they are aware of the figure's three-dimensional aspects, but do not understand how the drawing is related to the solid it depicts.

To understand how such a cube building is made, an adult might reason through the problem like this: How many cubes are in the first layer? How many layers are there? How many cubes are there in all? This strategy is natural for adults, but not for children. *Ruins of Montarek* could be viewed as a unit on "reading." Students read information from drawings to help them reason about three-dimensional objects, and they read three-dimensional objects to gather information to make two-dimensional representations.

Spatial visualization skills are very important in developing mathematical thinking and are critical to reading graphical information, using arrays and networks, and understanding the fundamental ideas of calculus. In the past several decades, research has raised many questions about spatial visualization abilities. Many studies have found that girls do not reason as well about spatial experiences as do boys, especially starting at about adolescence. The explanation offered by some psychologists, that this difference may be innate, is unacceptable to those of us concerned with teaching children.

In the mid-eighties, we conducted several studies of students who used the *Spatial Visualization* unit from the Middle Grades Mathematics Project. The studies examined whether experiences with building, observing, communicating spatial information, and representing three-dimensional objects could improve the performance of middle-school students—girls in particular—on tests of spatial visualization skills. One of the tests asked students to describe (on paper) a cube building so that a person reading the description would know exactly what the building looks like. Here are two isometric views of the building:

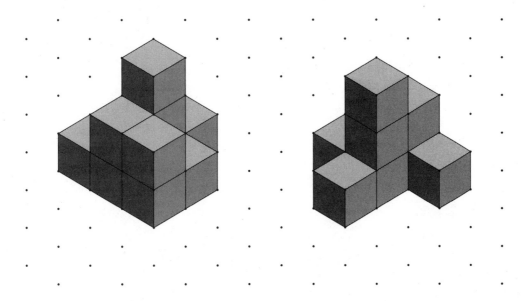

Below are two samples of student attempts before instruction. These students had great difficulty in successfully communicating spatial information.

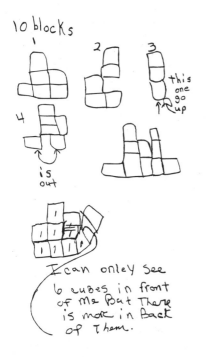

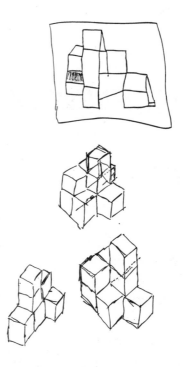

After instruction, most students were able to represent the building using the three forms of representation taught in the unit: a base plan, flat views (sets of building plans), and isometric views.

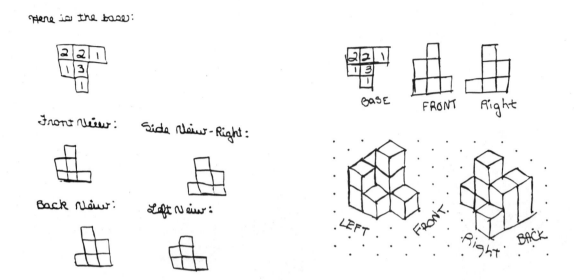

These studies clearly documented the benefits of such experiences. In fact, retention studies showed that students' abilities with spatial tasks had improved even more six weeks *after* the end of the unit! Students and teachers were interviewed to try to determine the cause of this amazing result. It was suspected that teachers might have followed the *Spatial Visualization* unit with a geometry unit, but this was not the case. However, the teachers did report that their students were still asking for isometric dot paper. The interviews with students were more revealing. One girl summed it up nicely: "Dr. Lappan, you have ruined my world—I see cubes everywhere!" The experiences had given students entirely new ways of viewing and interpreting their world.

The Mathematics in *Ruins of Montarek*

Spatial visualization is an important aspect of geometry and geometric reasoning, but it is often neglected or ignored completely in the middle-school mathematics curriculum. This unit develops students' spatial visualization skills through rich, hands-on problem situations. A variety of tools—including cubes, building plans, isometric dot paper, and two-dimensional cube models—are used in the activities. Students work with two- and three-dimensional representations of objects as they learn about the relationships between three-dimensional objects and their two-dimensional representations and about the limitations of representing three-dimensional objects in two-dimensions (for example, the representations don't always represent unique objects).

The major mathematical goals of this unit are for students to learn to construct, manipulate, and interpret two- and three-dimensional representations of objects and to develop an understanding of the relationships among different representations (such as building plans, isometric dot paper representations, and cube models). In other words, the unit is designed to help students learn to "read" and communicate information about three-dimensional objects from two-dimensional drawings, and to use two-dimensional representations to "write" about three-dimensional objects.

Two major representation schemes are developed in this unit: architectural views (elevations) and isometric dot paper representations. In architectural views, only one face of a building is shown in a drawing; in isometric drawings, three faces are shown. Several steps help to develop students' understanding of both major forms of representation:

1. Students are challenged to match cube buildings with drawings.

2. Students learn to make drawings that "capture" a building on paper.

3. Students learn to put together a building from a set of plans.

4. Students learn to construct and represent buildings and to evaluate the construction or representation of buildings.

As students work through these steps, they learn about the limitations of two-dimensional representations of three-dimensional objects. The question of uniqueness is raised: Can more than one building be constructed from a single set of plans? Students discover that both building plans and isometric drawings can "hide" cubes, so that it may not be possible to tell what certain parts of a building look like. Because the hidden parts may be completed in more than one way, several buildings may be possible from a set of building plans or an isometric drawing.

Students are also challenged to add constraints to building plans and isometric drawings so that they represent a unique building. They learn that this is possible for a set of building plans (by specifying that the building must be maximal) but impossible for an isometric representation.

Throughout the unit, questions are posed that require spatial reasoning beyond the "reading" involved in moving from cube buildings to drawings and vice versa. For example, in some problems students use clues to reason about how a building might look or to locate a room in a building with a particular view. Other problems involve reasoning about the ways incomplete building plans might be completed or about the least and greatest numbers of cubes that can be used to construct a building that fits a specific set of plans. Some students will develop analytic ways of thinking about such problems, such as looking at the building in layers, identifying cubes common to all buildings that fit a set of plans, or looking combinatorially at all possibilities. Other students will reason using mental visualization or mental rotation of the building. Through class discussion, students will hear about the spatial reasoning strategies of others and can then experiment with new strategies.

Unlike most other Connected Mathematics units, the assessment pieces for *Ruins of Montarek* include multiple-choice questions, which are very useful for testing visual discrimination and reasoning. Since students have not encountered multiple-choice questions in other units in the curriculum, an occasional multiple-choice item has been embedded in the ACE questions.

Ruins of Montarek **was created to help students**

- Read and create two-dimensional representations of three-dimensional cube buildings

- Communicate spatial information

- Observe that the back view of a cube building is the mirror image of the front view and that the left view is the mirror image of the right view

- Understand and recognize line symmetry

- Explain how drawings of the base outline, front view, and right view describe a building

- Construct cube buildings that fit two-dimensional building plans

- Develop a way to describe all buildings that can be made from a set of plans

- Understand that a set of plans can have more than one minimal building but only one maximal building

- Explain how a cube can be represented on isometric dot paper, how the angles on the cube are represented with angles on the dot paper, and how the representations fit what the eye sees when viewing the corner of a cube building

- Make isometric drawings of cube buildings

- Visualize transformations of cube buildings and make isometric drawings of the transformed buildings

- Reason about spatial relationships

- Use models and representations of models to solve problems

The overall goals of Connected Mathematics is to help students develop sound mathematical habits. Through their work in this and other geometry units, students learn important questions to ask themselves about any situation that can be represented and modeled mathematically, such as: *How can three-dimensional objects be shown in a two-dimensional world? How can a better understanding of space and solid figures be developed? How can imaging skills be developed by studying three-dimensional objects—such as buildings made from cubes? What is the value in studying an isometric drawing? a symmetric figure? minimum and maximum figures? How do these ideas help build visualization skills?*

Investigation 1: Building Plans

This investigation raises the question of what information an orthogonal view of a cube building gives the viewer. *Orthogonal views* are those made from directly in front of each face of a building, as if taken by a camera. Students develop these views of a cube building into a set of plans somewhat like architectural drawings.

Investigation 2: Making Buildings

In this investigation, students use plans to construct cube buildings. They discover that a set of building plans does not always correspond to a unique building. They also work with incomplete sets of plans to deepen their understanding of the contribution each drawing makes to a building.

Investigation 3: Describing Unique Buildings

In this investigation, students explore minimal and maximal buildings in search of a way to add a constraint to obtain a unique building from a set of building plans. They continue to develop their spatial reasoning and visualization skills.

Investigation 4: Isometric Dot Paper Representations

This investigation introduces students to isometric dot paper, which has dots arranged in a pattern useful for making drawings of cube buildings as viewed from a corner. Such *isometric drawings* show three faces of a cube building at the same time. Students build simple cube structures and visualize turning them into every position that can be drawn on isometric dot paper.

Investigation 5: Ziggurats

This investigation introduces students to a special kind of pyramid called a *ziggurat*. Students reflect on the forms of representation they have studied and analyze the strengths and weaknesses of each.

Investigation 6: Seeing the Isometric View

This final investigation focuses on the visualization of isometric views. Given several corner drawings of buildings, students are asked to identify to which building each drawing belongs. Students visualize and represent what a cube building would look like with specific cubes removed or new cubes added that touch certain faces. The unit closes with spatial puzzles in which students identify how a given building can be made from two basic shapes.

Connections to Other Units

The ideas in *Ruins of Montarek* build on and connect to several big ideas in other Connected Mathematics units.

Big Idea	Prior Work	Future Work
creating 2-D and 3-D representations and models of 3-D objects	exploring properties and measurements of 2-D figures; constructing models (with square tiles) of rectangular 2-D figures (*Shapes and Designs, Covering and Surrounding*)	finding surface area and volume of 3-D figures (*Filling and Wrapping*); studying and developing mathematical models, including linear, exponential, and quadratic equations, counting trees, and neworks (*Thinking with Mathematical Models, Clever Counting*)
exploring relationships between 2-D and 3-D representations of 3-D objects (includes uniqueness of representations, maximal and minimal buildings)	exploring uniqueness of prime factorization of integers (*Prime Time*); investigating relationships between polygons (*Shapes and Designs*)	working with 2-D sketches and diagrams of 3-D figures; using 3-D models to study 3-D figures, including cones, cylinders, spheres, prisms (*Filling and Wrapping*)
exploring symmetric properties of 2-D orthogonal views of 3-D cube buildings	exploring symmetry in 2-D shapes and polygons (*Shapes and Designs*)	exploring symmetry of graphs of functions (*Frogs, Fleas, and Painted Cubes*); exploring symmetry of shapes subject to isometries (*Hubcaps, Kaleidoscopes, and Mirrors!*)
interpreting and creating isometric views of 3-D objects	writing Logo programs that make specific shapes or shapes that meet specific conditions (*Shapes and Designs, Covering and Surrounding*)	visualizing and understanding properties of 3-D figures (e.g., cones, cylinders, spheres, prisms), including surface area as "wrapping" and volume as "filling" (*Filling and Wrapping*); visualizing growth patterns in exponential and quadratic functions, (*Growing, Growing, Growing, . . . , Frogs, Fleas, and Painted Cubes*)

Materials

For students

- Labsheets
- Cubes (20 per student; these are easy to manage if student sets are packaged in resealable plastic bags and if all cubes in a set are the same color)
- Sugar cubes (optional; see note below)
- Grid paper (provided as a blackline master)
- Isometric dot paper (provided as a blackline master)
- Rectangular dot paper (provided as a blackline master)
- Envelopes (1 per student)
- Straightedges
- Angle rulers
- Scissors

For the teacher

- Transparencies and transparency markers
- Transparencies of isometric dot paper and grid paper (copy the blackline masters onto blank transparency film)
- Interlocking cubes (optional)

Note: Many ACE questions require the use of cubes. If you cannot send cubes home with students, we recommend that students use sugar cubes for homework assignments.

Technology

We expect that students will use calculators freely to perform arithmetic computations so that their focus can be on analyzing the problems and searching for patterns. The Connected Mathematics curriculum was developed with the belief that calculators should always be available and that students should decide when to use them. For this reason, we do not designate specific problems as "calculator problems."

Pacing Chart

This pacing chart gives estimates of the class time required for each investigation and assessment piece. Shaded rows indicate opportunities for assessment.

Investigations and Assessments	Class Time
1 Building Plans	5 days
2 Making Buildings	3 days
3 Describing Unique Buildings	2 days
Check-Up 1	$\frac{1}{2}$ day
4 Isometric Dot Paper Representations	3 days
5 Ziggurats	3 days
6 Seeing the Isometric View	3 days
Check-Up 2	$\frac{1}{2}$ day
Quiz	1 day
Self-Assessment	Take home
Unit Test	1 day
Unit Project	1 day

Vocabulary

The following words and concepts are used in *Ruins of Montarek*. Concepts in the left column are those essential for student understanding of this and future units. The Descriptive Glossary gives descriptions of many of these and other words used in *Ruins of Montarek*.

Essential
base plan
set of building plans
maximal building
minimal building

Nonessential
building mat
isometric dot paper
ziggurat

Assessment Summary

Embedded Assessment

Opportunities for informal assessment of student progress are embedded throughout *Ruins of Montarek* in the problems, the ACE questions, and the Mathematical Reflections. Suggestions for observing as students explore and discover mathematical ideas, for probing to guide their progress in developing concepts and skills, and for questioning to determine their level of understanding can be found in the Launch, Explore, or Summarize sections of all investigation problems. Some examples:

- Investigation 5, Problem 5.1 *Launch* (page 71a) suggests how you can help your students understand the properties of a ziggurat.
- Investigation 1, Problem 1.2 *Explore* (page 25c) suggests how you might help students who are having trouble drawing mirror images.

■ Investigation 3, Problem 3.1 *Summarize* (page 51b) suggests questions you might ask to help students conduct a systematic search for all the buildings that fit a set of plans and then look for patterns in those buildings.

ACE Assignments

An ACE (Applications—Connections—Extensions) section appears at the end of each investigation. To help you assign ACE questions, a list of assignment choices is given in the margin next to the reduced student page for each problem. Each list indicates the ACE questions that students should be able to answer after they complete the problem.

Partner Quiz

One quiz, which may be given after Investigation 6, is provided with *Ruins of Montarek*. This quiz is designed to be completed by pairs of students with the opportunity for revision based on teacher feedback. You will find the quiz and its answers in the Assessment Resources section. As an alternative to the quiz provided, you can construct your own quizzes by combining questions from the Question Bank, the quiz, and unassigned ACE questions.

Check-Ups

Two check-ups, which may be given after Investigations 3 and 6, are provided for use as quick quizzes or warm-up activities. Check-ups are designed for students to complete individually. You will find the check-ups and their answer keys in the Assessment Resources section.

Question Bank

A Question Bank provides questions you can use for homework, reviews, or quizzes. You will find the Question Bank and its answer key in the Assessment Resources section.

Notebook/Journal

Students should have notebooks to record and organize their work. Notebooks should include student journals and sections for vocabulary, homework, and quizzes and check-ups. In their journals, students can take notes, solve investigation problems, write down ideas for their projects, and record their ideas about Mathematical Reflections questions. Journals should be assessed for completeness rather than correctness; they should be seen as "safe" places where students can try out their thinking. A Notebook Checklist and a Self-Assessment are provided in the Assessment Resources section. The Notebook Checklist helps students organize their notebooks. The Self-Assessment guides students as they review their notebooks to determine which ideas they have mastered and which they still need to work on.

The Unit Project: Design a Building

As a final assessment for *Ruins of Montarek*, you may assign the Unit Project, Design a Building, or you may administer the Unit Test. For the project, students imagine that they are architects in ancient Montarek. Each student must design a building that would be useful to the citizens of Montarek. A finished project will include a base plan, a set of building plans, four isometric sketches, and a letter explaining how the building would be used and how it would benefit the citizens of Montarek. A scoring rubric and a sample of student work are given in the Assessment Resources section.

The Unit Test

As a final assessment for *Ruins of Montarek*, you may administer the Unit Test, or you may assign the Unit Project. The test covers building plans and sketches that require isometric drawings.

Introducing Your Students to *Ruins of Montarek*

One way to introduce this unit is by discussing the questions on the opening spread of the student edition. Talk about situations in which we work with a representation of an object rather than with the object itself. Discuss both two- and three-dimensional representations. Globes and model kits are examples of three-dimensional representations. Video games, television images, photographs, and drawings are examples of two-dimensional representations.

You might discuss the difference between two- and three-dimensional objects in an informal way in terms of building a "frame" for an object. A two-dimensional object has no thickness and thus can be framed with a rectangle. A box is required to frame a three-dimensional object. The size of a rectangle is specified by giving two measures, length and width. Specifying the size of a box requires three measures: length, width, and height.

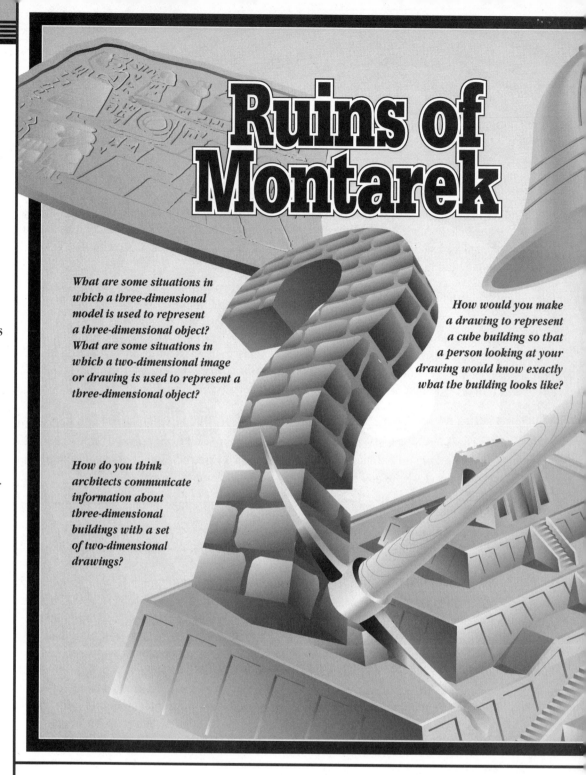

Ruins of Montarek

What are some situations in which a three-dimensional model is used to represent a three-dimensional object? What are some situations in which a two-dimensional image or drawing is used to represent a three-dimensional object?

How do you think architects communicate information about three-dimensional buildings with a set of two-dimensional drawings?

How would you make a drawing to represent a cube building so that a person looking at your drawing would know exactly what the building looks like?

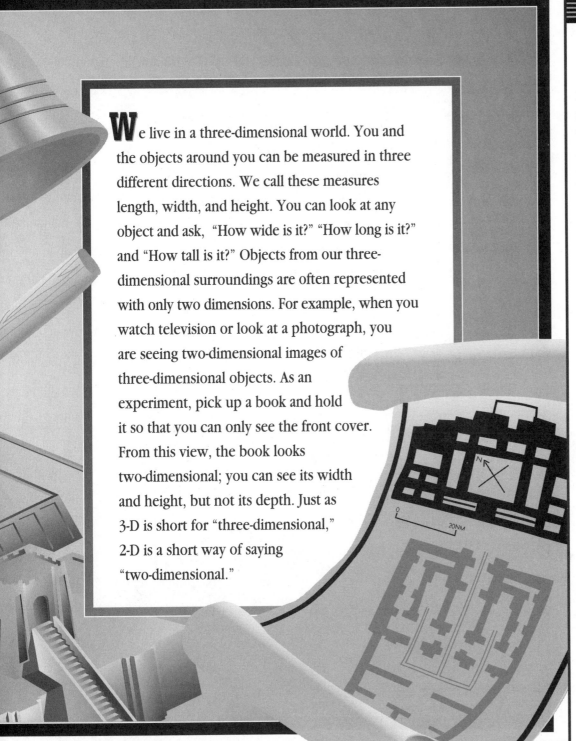

We live in a three-dimensional world. You and the objects around you can be measured in three different directions. We call these measures length, width, and height. You can look at any object and ask, "How wide is it?" "How long is it?" and "How tall is it?" Objects from our three-dimensional surroundings are often represented with only two dimensions. For example, when you watch television or look at a photograph, you are seeing two-dimensional images of three-dimensional objects. As an experiment, pick up a book and hold it so that you can only see the front cover. From this view, the book looks two-dimensional; you can see its width and height, but not its depth. Just as 3-D is short for "three-dimensional," 2-D is a short way of saying "two-dimensional."

Explain to students that in this unit they will be working with cube buildings and drawings that represent cube buildings. You might build a simple cube building and ask students for ideas about how to make a single drawing or several drawings to represent it. Explain that someone else should be able to construct the building by looking at the drawing or drawings.

You can then discuss the three problems on page 5 of the student edition. Explain that these are some of the types of questions students will answer in this unit. The point is not to solve the problems at this stage, but to get students interested in learning how to read and create representations of cube buildings. As you consider the ideas, ask students such questions as the following: What do you think this stands for? What do you think this tells you about the building? Why do you think the third problem has labels for front, back, left, and right?

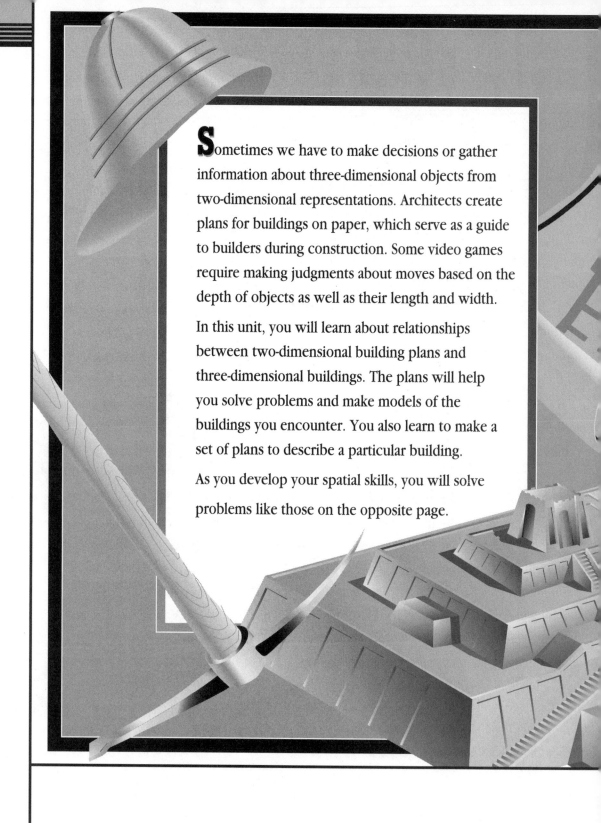

Sometimes we have to make decisions or gather information about three-dimensional objects from two-dimensional representations. Architects create plans for buildings on paper, which serve as a guide to builders during construction. Some video games require making judgments about moves based on the depth of objects as well as their length and width.

In this unit, you will learn about relationships between two-dimensional building plans and three-dimensional buildings. The plans will help you solve problems and make models of the buildings you encounter. You also learn to make a set of plans to describe a particular building.

As you develop your spatial skills, you will solve problems like those on the opposite page.

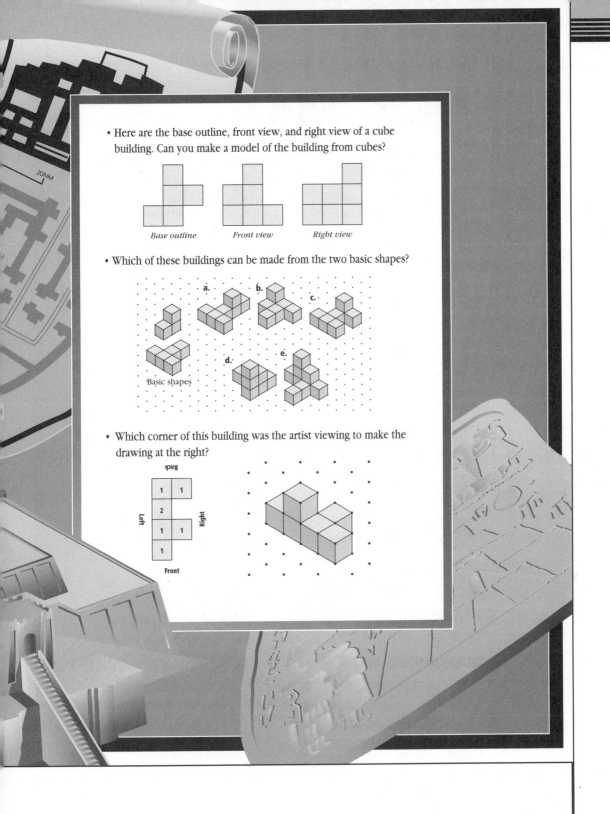

- Here are the base outline, front view, and right view of a cube building. Can you make a model of the building from cubes?

Base outline   *Front view*   *Right view*

- Which of these buildings can be made from the two basic shapes?

a.   b.   c.

Basic shapes   d.   e.

- Which corner of this building was the artist viewing to make the drawing at the right?

Back

1	1
2	
1	1
1	

Left   Right

Front

Mathematical Highlights

The Mathematical Highlights page provides information to students and to parents and other family members. It gives students a preview of the activities and problems in *Ruins of Montarek*. As they work through the unit, students can refer back to the Mathematical Highlights page to review what they have learned and to preview what is still to come. This page also tells students' families what mathematical ideas and activities will be covered as the class works through *Ruins of Montarek*.

Mathematical Highlights

In *Ruins of Montarek,* you will learn about three-dimensional buildings and their two-dimensional representations.

● As you match cube buildings with their building plans and draw plans that match a given building, you learn how two-dimensional drawings can be used to represent three-dimensional objects.

● Constructing all the possible cube buildings that fit a set of plans shows you that a set of building plans may not always describe a unique building.

● As you use the greatest and least possible numbers of cubes to construct buildings that fit a set of plans, you discover a constraint you can add to a set of building plans so that it defines a unique building.

● Isometric dot paper allows you to represent a building with a drawing that shows three views of the building at the same time.

● When you study buildings and their isometric drawings, you see how cubes can be "hidden" in isometric views of a building.

● Imagining what a cube building would look like if cubes were added or removed improves your visualization skills.

● Using a mirror to reflect figures helps you understand line symmetry.

● As you investigate clues, such as diary entries, you solve mysteries about ancient buildings.

Using a Calculator

In this unit, you will be able to use your calculator to help develop information for your unit project. As you work on the Connected Mathematics units, you decide whether to use a calculator to help you solve a problem.

The Investigations

The teaching materials for each investigation consist of three parts: an overview, student pages with teaching outlines, and detailed notes for teaching the investigation.

The overview of each investigation includes brief descriptions of the problems, the mathematical and problem-solving goals of the investigation, and a list of necessary materials.

Essential information for teaching the investigation is provided in the margins around the student pages. The "At a Glance" overviews are brief outlines of the Launch, Explore, and Summarize phases of each problem for reference as you work with the class. To help you assign homework, a list of "Assignment Choices" is provided next to each problem. Wherever space permits, answers to problems, follow-ups, ACE questions, and Mathematical Reflections appear next to the appropriate student pages.

The Teaching the Investigation section follows the student pages and is the heart of the Connected Mathematics curriculum. This section describes in detail the Launch, Explore, and Summarize phases for each problem. It includes all the information needed for teaching, along with suggestions for what you might say at key points in the teaching. Use this section to prepare lessons and as a guide for teaching an investigation.

Assessment Resources

The Assessment Resources section contains blackline masters and answer keys for the quiz, the check-ups, and the Question Bank. Blackline masters for the Notebook Checklist and the Self-Assessment are given. These instruments support student self-evaluation, an important aspect of assessment in the Connected Mathematics curriculum.

Blackline Masters

The Blackline Masters section includes masters for all labsheets and transparencies. Blackline masters of centimeter grid paper, dot paper, and isometric dot paper are also provided.

Additional Practice

Practice pages for each investigation offer additional problems for students who need more practice with the basic concepts developed in the investigations as well as some continual review of earlier concepts.

Descriptive Glossary

The Descriptive Glossary provides descriptions and examples of the key concepts in *Ruins of Montarek*. These descriptions are not intended to be formal definitions, but are meant to give you an idea of how students might make sense of these important concepts.

Index

The Index includes references to pages in both the student text and the teaching materials pages of this Teacher's Edition, which can be identified by their characteristic number-letter designations.

Building Plans

In this first investigation, students meet Emily Hawkins, an explorer and adventurer who is investigating the ruins of the fictitious city of Montarek. As Emily searches for clues about the lost city, students learn about the ways she interprets and represents her findings.

In Problem 1.1, Building from Base Plans, students are introduced to base plans as a simple way to represent cube buildings. After constructing a cube building from a base plan, they match the various views of the building to drawings in the text. In Problem 1.2, Reflecting Figures, students draw the reflections of figures over mirror lines. In Problem 1.3, Making Drawings of Cube Models, students build cube models and then sketch the various views. In Problem 1.4, Unraveling Mysteries, students draw the back and left views of a cube building based on the front and right views. They learn that the front view is the mirror image of the back and that the left view is the mirror image of the right; therefore, only one view from each pair is necessary for visually describing a building. In Problem 1.5, Matching a Building to Its Plans, students identify the plans that match a given building. In Problem 1.6, Which Building Is Which? students match four buildings with their building plans. They also begin to see that more than one cube building can sometimes be made from a set of building plans.

Mathematical and Problem-Solving Goals

- *To look at a cube building and see the orthogonal views without being distracted by depth perception*

- *To understand and use line symmetry (mirror symmetry)*

- *To discover that the base outline and the front and right views can be used to represent a cube building*

- *To draw sets of plans for cube buildings*

- *To match buildings to sets of building plans*

Materials		
Problem	For students	For the teacher
All	Calculator, cubes (20 per student), building mat (make these in Problem 1.1), grid paper, sugar cubes (optional; for homework)	Transparencies 1.1A to 1.6B (optional)
1.2	Labsheets 1.2A and 1.2B (1 per student), mirror or other reflecting device	
ACE	Labsheet 1.ACE	

Building Plans

Have you ever seen a building under construction? As a building crew is constructing a building, they use a set of building plans. *Building plans* show how the different parts of the building—such as the foundation, walls, and ceilings—fit together. Building plans are created by architects and used by building crews and construction supervisors.

In this unit, you will learn about drawings that show what the base and the outside of a building look like. You will also use sets of building plans to construct models of buildings out of cubes. Models tell you how much space is in the building and what it looks like from the outside.

In this unit, Emily Hawkins, a famous explorer and adventurer, investigates the ancient ruins of the lost city of Montarek. As she explores the ruins, Emily finds it helpful to make models of the buildings from cubes. Some of the buildings that once existed in the city are now gone, so making models from the clues that remain is the *only* way to study them.

Building from Base Plans

At a Glance

Grouping:
Pairs

Launch

- Have students make building mats.

- From the given base plan, have each student construct the cube building.

Explore

- As students work on the problem, help them understand orthogonal views.

- Ask partners to share answers and then work on follow-up questions 1–4.

- Assign follow-up question 5 for students who are ready for a challenge.

Summarize

- Discuss the problem and follow-up, making sure students understand that the back and front views, and the left and right views, are mirror images.

Assignment Choices

1.1 Building from Base Plans

The following problems will introduce you to how Emily Hawkins uses sets of plans to describe buildings. You will need 15 cubes and a building mat. A *building mat* is a sheet of paper labeled "Front," "Back," "Left," and "Right" as shown below.

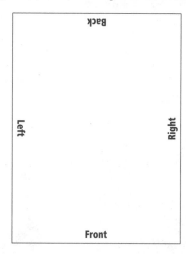

When you make your building mat, put the labels near the edges so there is a large area inside the labels. Always have the building mat on your desk so that the word "Front" is toward you.

One important piece of information to have about a building is the base outline. A *base outline* is a drawing of the building's base. The base outline tells you the shape of the building's base and how many cubes are in the bottom layer. In Problem 1.1, you will be working with a building with this base outline:

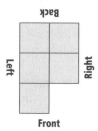

One kind of plan for a building is a simple base plan. A **base plan** is a drawing of the base with numbers on the squares to show how high each stack of cubes is. The building you will be working with in Problem 1.1 has this base plan:

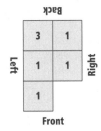

Problem 1.1

The drawings above show the base outline and the base plan for a building. Use the base outline to construct the first layer of the building on your building mat.

How many cubes do you need to construct the bottom layer?

Now use the base plan to complete the building.

If you turn the building mat so that you look at the front, back, left, or right side of your cube building straight on, you will see a two-dimensional pattern of squares. Turn the building on your mat and decide which side of the building (front, back, left, or right) Emily was looking at when she made these diagrams:

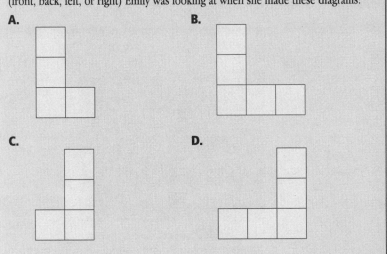

Answers to Problem 1.1

A.   front

B.   left

C.   back

D.   right

Reflecting Figures

Launch

- Help students use a reflecting device to see the reflection of a figure over a mirror line.

Explore

- As pairs work on the problem, help them understand mirror images.

- Ask students with a good understanding of the problem to help those who are struggling.

Summarize

- Discuss the problem, making sure students understand how to draw the mirror image of a figure.

- With the class, explore figures that have line symmetry.

- Have the class work on the follow-up

Assignment Choices

ACE questions 16 and 17 (these questions require Labsheet 1.ACE)

■ **Problem 1.1 Follow-Up**

1. Compare the four views. What relationships do you see among them? How are they alike and how are they different?

2. If you are on one side of a cube model of a building and your friend is on the opposite side, how do your views of the cube model compare?

3. If your friend shows you a drawing of the back view of a cube model of a building, can you draw the front view? Why or why not?

4. Below is the view of a cube model of a building from the right. What does the left view look like?

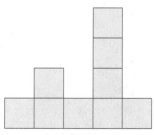

Right view

5. Create a building on your building mat that has the right view shown in question 4. Draw the views from the other three sides of your building. Have your partner check your building and views while you check your partner's.

1.2 Reflecting Figures

A small mirror is useful for visualizing the opposite sides of cube models. You can use a mirror to see the reflection, or *mirror image*, of a given view of a building.

The Washington Monument and its reflection in the Tidal Basin

---

Answers to Problem 1.1 Follow-Up

1. Possible answer: The front view is the mirror image of the back view, and the left view is the mirror image of the right view.

2. The views are mirror images of each other.

3. yes; The front view is the mirror image of the back view.

4. The left view is the mirror image of the right view.   5.   Answers will vary.

Left view

Problem 1.2

Labsheet 1.2A shows the figures below. For each drawing, set the edge of a mirror on the mirror line so that the reflecting surface is facing the cube diagram. Sketch the mirror image on the other side of the mirror line, and label the image. If the image is the opposite of the *front,* it must be the *back.* If it is the opposite of the *right,* it must be the *left.*

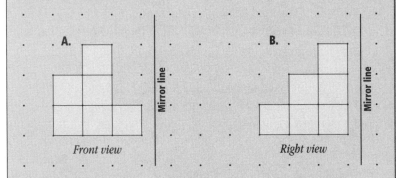

Labsheet 1.2A also shows the polygons below. Try to imagine what the mirror image of each figure would look like. On the labsheet, draw what you think the image will look like. Use a mirror to check your prediction.

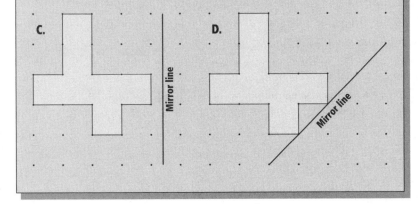

Answers to Problem 1.2

A.

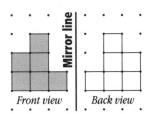

B.

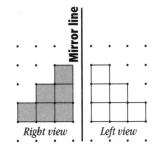

C.   See page 25i.

D.   See page 25i.

■ Problem 1.2 Follow-Up

If you made the drawings in Problem 1.2 correctly, they will show *line symmetry* around the mirror line. This means that if you fold your paper on the mirror line, the figure fits exactly on top of its image. Sometimes you can draw a mirror line on the figure itself. If you fold the figure on the mirror line, its two parts fall exactly on top of each other.

1. On Labsheet 1.2B, see if you can draw mirror lines on the figures shown below.

a. 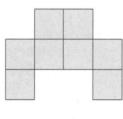   **b.**

2. How many different mirror lines can you find for this figure? Use the figure on Labsheet 1.2B and a mirror to test your ideas.

Answers to Problem 1.2 Follow-Up

1. a.

1. b.

2. See page 25i.

1.3 Making Drawings of Cube Models

You can represent a cube building by drawing the base outline and the front, back, left, and right views of the building.

Problem 1.3

Construct this building on your building mat.

A. Draw the base outline of the building on a piece of grid paper. Remember that the base outline shows the cubes that touch the building mat. Then, draw and label the front, back, left, and right views.

```
        ┌───┐
        │ 3 │
    ┌───┼───┤
    │ 2 │ 1 │
    └───┴───┘
      Front
```

B. Remove a cube from the building. Draw a base outline and a set of views for the new building.

C. Return the cube you removed so that you again have the original building. Now, add three more cubes to the building. Draw a base outline and a set of views for the new building.

▦ Problem 1.3 Follow-Up

Look carefully at your views for each building. For each set of views, do you see any relationships that would let you use fewer views to represent the same information about the building?

Did you know?

The area that is now Central America and southern Mexico was once the home of an ancient people called the Maya. The Mayan civilization flourished between A.D. 250 and A.D. 900. The Maya made extraordinary advancements in astronomy, mathematics, and architecture. Mayan architects created remarkable buildings, including tall limestone pyramids topped by temples, like the one shown at right. Priests climbed the stairs of these pyramids and performed ceremonies in the temples.

▬ ▬ ▬ At a Glance ▬ ▬ ▬

**Grouping:
Individuals or Pairs**

Launch

■ If students understand the mirror-image relationship between front and back views and between right and left views, use this problem as a summary.

■ Distribute transparent grids on which students can record their work. (*optional*)

Explore

■ As students work, help them to visualize the different views of a building.

■ Look for interesting solutions to parts B and C.

Summarize

■ As a class, share solutions to the problem.

■ Have the class work on the follow-up.

Answers to Problem 1.3

See page 25j.

Answer to Problem 1.3 Follow-Up

Since the back view is the mirror image of the front view, it is only necessary to show one of these views. Similarly, since the left view is the mirror image of the right view, it is only necessary to show one of these views.

Assignment Choices

ACE question 8 and unassigned choices from earlier problems

Unraveling Mysteries

Launch

■ As a class, do parts A and B of the problem.

■ After students work individually, they may work in groups on parts C and D.

Explore

■ As students explore whether more than one building fits the drawings, look for interesting insights and conjectures.

■ Distribute transparent grids on which groups can record their base plan. (*optional*)

Summarize

■ In a class discussion, have students share their ideas and their buildings.

1.4 Unraveling Mysteries

Emily Hawkins is trying to unravel some old mysteries about the ruins of the ancient city of Montarek (pronounced *mon tar´ek*). At the site of the ruins, she discovered pieces of broken stone tablets that have parts of sketches and diagrams etched on them. Emily needs to decipher the etchings to reconstruct the entire set of diagrams and sketches.

Problem 1.4

Some of the stone fragments show the front and right views of a building from the ancient city of Montarek.

A. The etchings show this front view of the building:

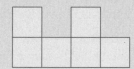

On your grid paper, draw the back view.

B. The etchings show this right view of the building:

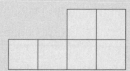

On your grid paper, draw the left view.

C. Use your cubes to build a building that matches your four views.

D. Do you think there is more than one building with the front and right views etched on the tablets and the back and left views you have sketched on grid paper? Explain your answer.

■ **Problem 1.4 Follow-Up**

Describe in *words* how what you see looking at a cube building from the front compares to what you see looking at the cube building from the back.

Assignment Choices

ACE questions 11, 12–15 (as an extra challenge), and unassigned choices from earlier problems

Answers to Problem 1.4

A.

B.

C. Possible answer:

	1	2	1
2	1	2	
1	1	1	
1	1	1	1

Front

D. Possible answer: There is more than one building. I know this because I could add another cube to my building and it would still fit the drawings.

1.5 Matching a Building to Its Plans

In the last problem, you found that the right view of a cube building is the mirror image of the left view. Once you see the right view of a cube building, the left view does not give you any new information. Therefore, the plans for a cube building need only contain one of these views. For the same reason, a set of plans need only contain the front view or the back view, not both.

When Emily refers to a **set of building plans,** she is talking about a set of three diagrams—the front view, the right view, and the base outline.

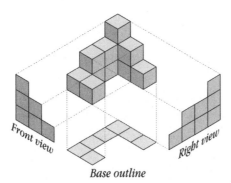

Front view

Right view

Base outline

Problem 1.5

Emily found a fragment of a stone tablet with this base plan etched on it:

Front

On your building mat, construct the building represented by the base plan.

Emily also found the three sets of building plans shown on the next page on stone tablets. Does one of the three sets of plans correspond to the building you made using the base plan? If so, which one?

Investigation 1: Building Plans 15

Answer to Problem 1.4 Follow-Up

See page 25j.

Answer to Problem 1.5

Set 3 is the correct set of plans.

1.5

Matching a Building to Its Plans

At a Glance

Grouping:
Individuals

Launch

■ Have each student construct a building from the given base plan.

■ Have students work individually on the problem.

Explore

■ As students determine which set of plans corresponds to their building, remind them to be able to explain why the other building plans are incorrect.

Summarize

■ In a class discussion, ask students to share their answers and their strategies for solving the problem.

Assignment Choices

ACE questions 1–4, 9, 10, and unassigned choices from earlier problems

Investigation 1 15

Which Building Is Which?

Launch

- Explain that each student in the group should build one of the buildings, and that every student should match each of the group's buildings to a set of plans.

Explore

- After each student in a group has looked at every building, the group should check answers and resolve any differences.

- Assign ACE questions 5–7 and 12–14 as challenges for groups who finish early. (*optional*)

Summarize

- Have a few students share strategies for matching buildings and building plans.

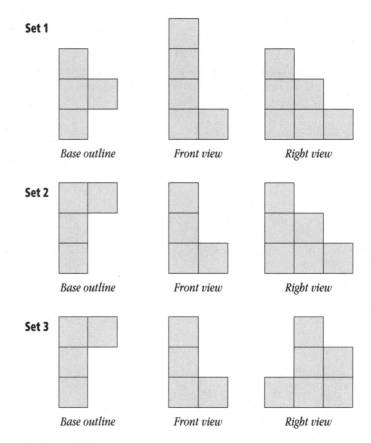

Set 1

Base outline   Front view   Right view

Set 2

Base outline   Front view   Right view

Set 3

Base outline   Front view   Right view

■ **Problem 1.5 Follow-Up**

Examine the sets of plans that do not match the building. Explain why each of these sets of plans does not match.

 1.6 **Which Building Is Which?**

In this problem, you will have a chance to test your observation skills. You will try to match four different buildings with their building plans. In order to "read" information about buildings from drawings, you need to be very observant and look carefully at both the drawings and the building.

Assignment Choices

ACE questions 5–7 and unassigned choices from earlier problems

Answer to Problem 1.5 Follow-Up

Set 1 has an incorrect base outline, the stack of four cubes in the front view is too high, and the right view shows stacks of height 3, 2, and 1 instead of 1, 3, and 2. Set 2 has the correct base outline and front view but the same incorrect right view as set 1.

Problem 1.6

Below are base plans for four different buildings. With your group, construct a
model of each building on a building mat.

A.

2	1	2
2	3	
2	1	

Front

B.

1	1	2
3	1	
2	1	

Front

C.

2	1	1
3	2	
1	1	

Front

D.

1	2	1
2	3	
1	1	

Front

Now, use your observation skills to match your buildings with the drawings on the
next page. When you are finished, discuss your ideas with your group and try to
reach consensus about which views go with which building.

■ **Problem 1.6 Follow-Up**

1. Can you remove cubes from the building in part A without changing its building plans?
   Explain your answer.
2. Can you remove cubes from the building in part B without changing its building plans?
   Explain your answer.
3. Can you remove cubes from the building in part C without changing its building plans?
   Explain your answer.
4. Can you remove cubes from the building in part D without changing its building
   plans? Explain your answer.

Answer to Problem 1.6

The building in part A matches set 3, the building in part B matches set 1, the building in
part C matches set 4, and the building in part D matches set 2.

Answers to Problem 1.6 Follow-Up

1. For building A, you could remove
   cubes from two spots.

   You can
   remove one
   or both of
   these cubes.

1	1	2
1	3	
2	1	

   Front

2. No cubes can be removed.

3. See page 25k.

4. See page 25k.

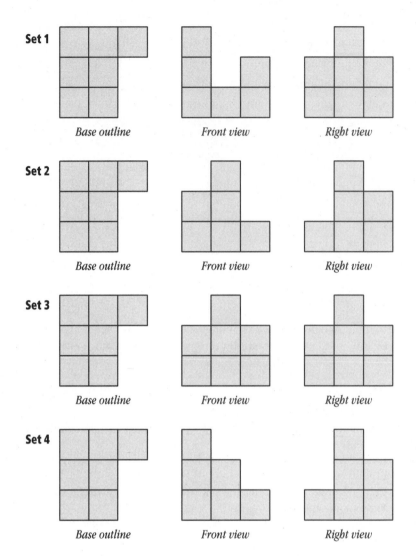

Set 1

Base outline   Front view   Right view

Set 2

Base outline   Front view   Right view

Set 3

Base outline   Front view   Right view

Set 4

Base outline   Front view   Right view

Applications · Connections · Extensions

As you work on these ACE questions, use your calculator whenever you need it.

Applications

In 1–4, make a cube model of the building represented by the base plan. Then, make a set of building plans for the building on grid paper. Remember that a *set of building plans* includes a base outline and the front and right views of the building.

1.

1	1	1
1	1	
2		

Front

2.

2	2	1
	3	1
		1

Front

3.

2	1	1
	3	1
	2	

Front

4.

2	3	1
	1	2
	1	

Front

In 5–7, make a cube model of the building represented by the base plan. Then, match the building with the correct set of plans.

5.

1	1	1	1
2	3	3	
	2		

Front

6.

1	3	2	3
1	2	1	
	1		

Front

4.

Base outline

Right view

Front view

5. set B

6. set C

Answers

Applications

1.

Base outline

Front view

Right view

2.

Base outline

Front view

Right view

3.

Base outline

Front view

Right view

7. set A

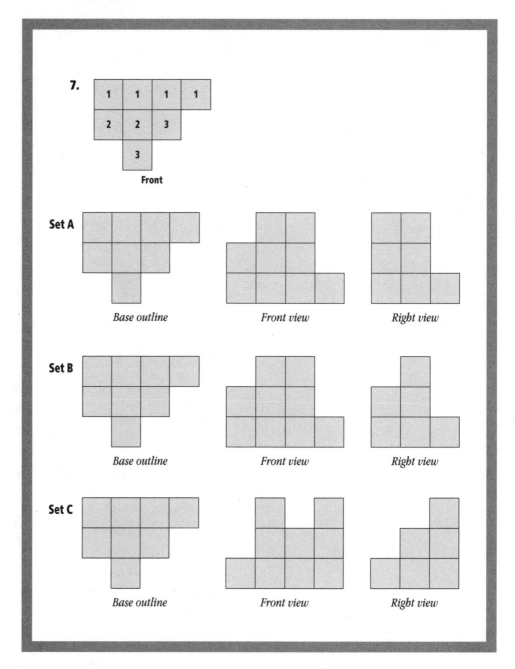

8. Each side of a number cube is numbered 1, 2, 3, 4, 5, or 6. The numbers are placed so that opposite sides add to 7. Below is the outline of a number cube with some values marked. What should the values of a, b, and c be so that the outline will fold up into a number cube?

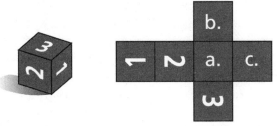

Connections

In 9 and 10, look back at the building plans you made in ACE questions 1 and 3.

9. If the length of a side of each square shown on your building plans is 1 unit, what is the perimeter of each of the three diagrams—base outline, front view, and right view—in each set of building plans for ACE questions 1 and 3?

10. If you were to paint the *top* of each exposed cube on the cube model in ACE question 1, how many square units would you have to paint?

8a. 6
8b. 4
8c. 5

Connections

9. See page 25k.

10. 6 square units (The number of squares on the base is the same as the area to be painted.)

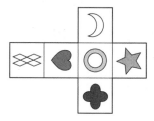

Extensions

11a. Answers will vary. Arranging the eight cubes in a single layer would create lots of floor space.

11b. A stack of eight cubes is the highest tower possible.

12. Possible answer:

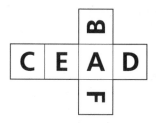

13.

Extensions

11. Emily Hawkins says that in the ancient city of Montarek, different kinds of buildings served different purposes. For example, some buildings were constructed to be garden houses, and others were built to be watchtowers.

    a. Garden houses needed lots of floor space so plants could be displayed and people would have room to walk through the gardens. Draw a base plan for a building that uses eight cubes that you think best meets this requirement for lots of floor space.

    b. Watchtowers needed to be tall but did not need much floor space. Draw a base plan for a building that uses eight cubes that you think would best suit the requirements for a watchtower.

In 12–14, three views of a cube and a sketch of a flattened cube are shown. Copy the sketch of the flattened cube on a sheet of grid paper. Then, use information from the pictures to mark the squares so that, if you folded the sketch into a cube, it would match the drawings.

12.

  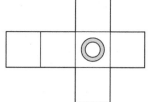

13.

   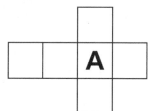

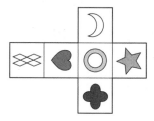

14.

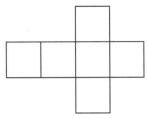

15. Design a cube puzzle of your own.

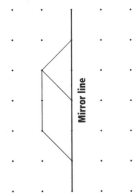

In 16 and 17, use Labsheet 1.ACE. Complete each diagram so that it has line symmetry around the mirror line shown.

16.

Mirror line

14.

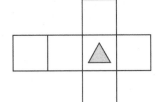

15. Answers will vary.

16.

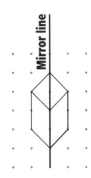

Mirror line

17. See below right.

18. Answers will vary.

17.

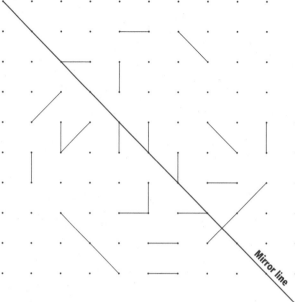

18. Design a figure on dot paper that has at least one line of symmetry.

17.

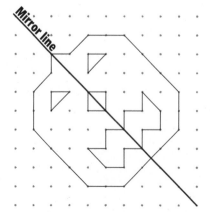

Mathematical Reflections

In this investigation, you have been learning to read information about three-dimensional buildings from two-dimensional drawings. These questions will help you summarize what you have learned:

(1) How does what you see looking at the front of a cube model compare to what you see looking at the back of the cube model?

(2) What does it mean for a figure to have *line symmetry?* Give an example as a part of your explanation.

(3) How many lines of symmetry does a 3-sided regular polygon have? A 4-sided regular polygon? A 5-sided regular polygon? A 12-sided regular polygon? How do you know your answers are correct?

(4) Why is it possible to describe a building with a set of only three drawings—the base outline, the front view, and the right view—rather than a set of views showing each of the four sides and a base outline?

Think about your answers to these questions, discuss your ideas with other students and your teacher, and then write a summary of your findings in your journal.

Tips for the Linguistically Diverse Classroom

Diagram Code The Diagram Code technique is described in detail in *Getting to Know Connected Mathematics*. Students use a minimal number of words and drawings, diagrams, or symbols to respond to questions that require writing. Example: Question 1—A student might answer this question by drawing a mirror, labeled with the words *mirror image*, between the front and back views of a cube building.

Possible Answers

1. The front of a cube model is the mirror image of the back. For example, if the front view has a stack of three cubes on the left, the back view will have a stack of three cubes on the right.

2. See page 25l.

3. A regular polygon with 3 sides has 3 lines of symmetry. A regular polygon with 4 sides has 4 lines of symmetry. A regular polygon with 5 sides has 5 lines of symmetry. A regular polygon with 12 sides has 12 lines of symmetry. (**Teaching Tip:** All regular polygons with an even number of sides have two types of lines of symmetry: one formed by connecting opposite vertices, the other formed by connecting the midpoints of opposite sides. In regular polygons with an odd number of sides, lines of symmetry are formed by connecting each vertex to the midpoint of the opposite side. In either case, there are as many lines of symmetry as there are sides (or vertices).)

4. Since the back view is the mirror image of the front view and the left view is the mirror image of the right view, the back and left views provide no additional information.

TEACHING THE INVESTIGATION

1.1 • Building from Base Plans

As this unit is highly visual, an overhead projector and transparencies of the problems would be extremely helpful. Transparencies of grid paper and, for a later investigation, isometric dot paper will also be useful.

Launch

Read or describe the information on page 7 of the investigation, which sets the scene by focusing students on thinking like architects and builders.

Have each student make a building mat by labeling a blank sheet of paper as shown in the student edition.

> The paper you have just labeled is called a *building mat.* The front of the building mat should be facing you. Always build your cube buildings in the center of the mat, with the building oriented so that the front of the building faces the front of the building mat. By carefully turning the building mat, you can look at your buildings from all sides without knocking them over.

Refer students to page 8 of the student edition, display the base outline on Transparency 1.1A, or draw the base outline below on the board.

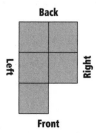

> This is the base outline of a cube building. The *base outline* shows you the shape of the base of a building and exactly what the bottom layer of cubes looks like. Build this layer on your mat.

Now refer students to the base plan shown on the top of page 9 in their books, display the base plan on Transparency 1.1A, or draw the base plan below on the board.

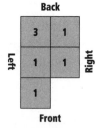

> This is the base plan for the building. The *base plan* looks like the base outline, but it has a number on each square. What do you think the numbers mean?

Students will probably correctly suggest that the numbers indicate the number of cubes in each stack. However, there may be confusion about whether the numbers include the bottom cubes. Make sure students understand that each number represents the total number of cubes in the stack, *including* the bottom cube.

> Add cubes to your base to make a cube building that matches this base plan.

> Now bend down so that your eye is level with the building. Look at the building straight on, from directly in front of one of its sides.

Refer students to Problem 1.1 in their books or display Transparency 1.1B.

> In this problem, you need to match each of these drawings with a side of your building. These drawings are flat; they do not have depth. Closing one eye will help you to see like a camera, which does not see depth.

Explore

As students work, circulate to help them learn to look at the *orthogonal views*, views made straight on in front of each side of an object.

As students finish working on the problem, ask them to compare their answers with their partner's and then to answer follow-up questions 1 through 4. You can use follow-up question 5 as an extension for students who are ready. Challenge students to build and make base plans for several buildings that have the given right view.

Summarize

As a class, discuss the answers to the problem and follow-up. Be sure students understand that the front view is the mirror image of the back view and the left view is the mirror image of the right view. One dramatic way to demonstrate this is to put the image of the right view from the follow-up on a transparency and then flip the transparency to show the left view.

Have several students display the base plans for the buildings they created for follow-up question 5, which demonstrates that many buildings can have the identical right view.

1.2 • Reflecting Figures

This problem builds on the observation made in Problem 1.1: the back view is the mirror image of the front view, and the left view is the mirror image of the right view. In this problem, mirrors are used to connect this concept to the idea of line symmetry, which was introduced in the *Shapes and Designs* unit.

Launch

Each student or pair will need a reflecting device, such as a small mirror or an index card wrapped with aluminum foil.

Distribute a copy of Labsheet 1.2A to each student.

> On Labsheet 1.2A, you see several figures drawn on dot paper. Next to each figure is a *mirror line*. In this problem, you will find the mirror image of each figure and then draw the image on the other side of the mirror line.

Demonstrate how to set a mirror on the indicated line, perpendicular to the page, with the reflecting surface facing the figure. Have students follow your actions at their desks, and make sure they all can see the reflection of the image in the mirror.

> What does the mirror do to the object being reflected? (*It flips it over. It turns it so that it faces the other way.*)

When students understand what to do, let them work in pairs on the problem.

Explore

Some students will find this problem a challenge. Ask students who show understanding to help those who are struggling with their drawings. Sometimes it helps to focus attention on the vertices of the drawings.

> (*Point to a vertex on the figure.*) Where is the image of this point on the reflection of the figure?

The image of a point is on the line that runs through the point, perpendicular to the mirror line. The image is the same distance from the mirror line as the point, but on the opposite side.

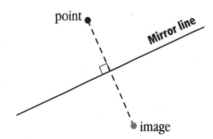

Summarize

As a class, discuss the answers to the problem. Ask several students to explain their techniques for drawing the mirror images.

> Look carefully at your drawings. Describe the figures on each side of the mirror line. How do they compare to each other? (*They are the same, only flipped.*)

> What would happen if you folded the paper on the mirror line? (*The figure would match exactly with the image.*)

On the board or overhead, show a simple figure and its reflection over a line.

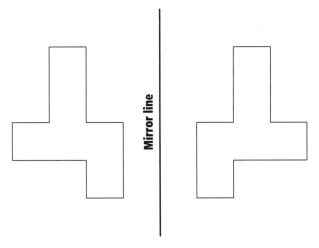

Mirror line

> This drawing shows *symmetry* about the mirror line. This means that if
> I folded the paper on the line, the two figures would match up exactly.
>
> Sometimes you can draw a mirror line on the figure itself.

Show an equilateral triangle on the board or overhead.

> Could you draw a line so that, if the triangle were folded on the line,
> the parts would match up exactly? (*Yes, we could draw a line from a
> vertex to the center of the opposite side.*) This means that the figure
> has line symmetry (or folding symmetry).

Have students work on the follow-up questions and compare their work with a partner's. When
students have finished, discuss the answers to the follow-up.

1.3 • Making Drawings of Cube Models

Just as writing their own stories improves students' comprehension of written stories, drawing
building plans deepens their skills in "reading" building plans. By drawing their own plans, students will better understand how the base outline and the views relate and why building plans
must be drawn in a consistent way. For example, the base outline is always drawn with the front
forward so one can see how the front and right views fit onto the base. To visualize the three
parts working together, students must picture the base in a horizontal plane and the front and
right views in vertical planes.

Launch

By now you will have a sense of how well your students understand the mirror-image relationship between the front and back views and the right and left views. If you think everyone is comfortable, use Problem 1.3 as a summary. Pace students quickly through parts A, B, and C, having
everyone remove or add the same cubes. Ask questions after each part to focus students on the
mirror-image relationships.

If you feel your students are not yet comfortable with mirror-image relationships, do part A as a class and then have them work individually or in pairs on the rest of the problem, choosing for themselves which cubes to add or remove. This allows them time to make sense of these ideas, and allows you to assist students who are struggling. You may want to give each individual or pair a transparent grid on which to record their work to make reporting to the class easier.

Explore

As students work, help those who are still having trouble visualizing the different views of the buildings. Look for especially interesting buildings created for parts B and C.

Summarize

If you pace the class through the problem, this summary occurs after each part as you have students share their answers and look for relationships.

> Let's begin by having a pair show us their work on part B. (*Choose a pair to report.*) Do you notice any relationships among the four views— front, back, right, and left? (*Yes; the front and back views are mirror images, and the left and right views are mirror images.*)

> Now let's look at part C. (*Choose a pair to show their work.*) Tell us what you observed about your drawings of the four views. (*The front and back views are mirror images, as are the right and left views.*)

> The follow-up asks you to find a way to give the same information about a building with fewer views. Think about this yourself for a minute. Then, share your ideas with your partner.

Give the class a few minutes to consider the question.

> Let's hear some ideas. What do you think we could do? (*We could draw either the front view or the back view; we don't need both. Similarly, we could draw either the right view or the left view.*)

Make sure students understand that this works because if you have one of the views, you can draw the other if you need it.

1.4 • Unraveling Mysteries

This problem gives students more practice drawing plans and constructing buildings from a set of plans.

Launch

Consider parts A and B of the problem as a class. Display Transparency 1.4, or refer students to the drawing of the front view in the student edition, and ask them to draw the back view on grid paper. Next, refer them to the right view and ask them to draw the left view. Check that students have made correct drawings. Then launch parts C and D, which address the main goal of the problem.

> You now have drawings of all four views of the building Emily is trying to reconstruct. Your challenge is to build a cube building that matches these four drawings.

Ask students to work individually and then share their ideas with their groups. Remind groups to be prepared to talk about and illustrate what they have found.

Explore

In their groups, students should determine whether there is more than one building that matches the drawings. Look for interesting insights and conjectures from the groups about which buildings fit the four drawings. You may want to give each group a transparent grid so they can make base plans for their buildings to share during the summary. When students finish the problem, have them work on the follow-up.

Summarize

In a class discussion, ask groups to share their ideas and strategies for constructing the buildings. Encourage them to discuss their strategies for constructing buildings from the information given in the views. Have them display their buildings so the class can see them.

Here are some ways students may approach making their buildings:

- Some students build a representation of the front view that is one cube thick. When they realize that they must fit the right view onto this stack, they begin to use information from all the views to construct the base.

- Some students look back and forth between the front and right views to discern what the base could look like. (Occasionally, even this early in the unit, a student recognizes that the base can be no wider than the front view and no longer than the right view, so a base that is four cubes by four cubes will work and will be the largest base that will work.)

- Some students try to use as many cubes as they can; others try to use the least possible number of cubes.

- Some students have trouble with cubes in front of taller stacks, a difficulty that appears both in their drawings and in their attempts to build from views. It is hard for them to recognize that a stack of two cubes in the front view does not necessarily indicate a stack of two cubes in the frontmost section of the building.

Discuss the answer to the follow-up question.

This quick activity, which students can do individually, prepares students for the matching activity in the next problem. This problem and the next give students practice in reading building plans. In this problem, students are given a building and must determine which set of plans matches the building.

Launch

Refer students to page 15, or display Transparency 1.5A.

> On your building mat, make a building from this given base plan.

When each student has made the correct building, present the problem.

> You are given three sets of building plans. Your job is to determine which, if any, of the plans matches your building.

Explore

As students work, remind them to be prepared to explain why each set of plans that does not match their building is incorrect.

Summarize

Call on a student to give an answer to the problem; check to see whether the class agrees. If there are differences of opinion, ask students to present evidence until the class agrees on an answer.

Ask students to discuss their strategies for deciding which plans fit the building. You can encourage them to think about strategies by asking questions like these:

> Which of the views did you check first? Why?

> What did you check next?

> How can you verify your answer?

Here are some strategies students have described:

■ Miriam checked the base first. From this she determined that the building matched either set 2 or set 3.

■ Tai checked the front first. From this he determined that the building matched either set 2 or set 3.

■ Arthur said he thought the building should have a front view like the one in set 1 because, since the building had one cube in front of the stack of three cubes, the front view should show a stack of four cubes. (He is having trouble understanding that the orthogonal view does not show cubes in front of other cubes.)

■ After narrowing the choices to sets 2 and 3, Tai eliminated set 2 because the right view shows three cubes in the first stack. A correct set of plans must show one cube in this stack. Tai then verified that all the views in set 3 matched the building.

1.6 • Which Building Is Which?

This activity is the culmination of the lessons directed toward observation. Students must be very comfortable with the methods of representing buildings in order to be successful in the lessons that follow.

Launch

Refer students to Problem 1.6 in their books, or display Transparency 1.6A.

> You have already passed the first stage of becoming an explorer and adventurer like Emily Hawkins. You have figured out what views are needed to represent a cube building. You have drawn plans for a building, and you have successfully matched a set of plans to a building.
>
> In this problem, you face a greater challenge! You will work with your group to build four buildings that are more complex than the building in the last problem. Then you will try to match each building with its building plans.

Explain that the problem gives base plans for four buildings, and that each person in each group should build one of the buildings.

> After you make your building, study it carefully. Try to figure out which of the four sets of plans shown on page 18 matches your building. Then, swap buildings with someone else in your group, and find a match for the new building. Continue until you have looked at all four buildings.

You may want to suggest to students that it is much easier to move people than it is to move buildings.

> When everyone in your group has finished, check your answers and resolve any differences. Be prepared to talk about why you think you are correct.

Explore

Some groups will finish this activity quickly; others will need more time. ACE questions 5–7 are good extensions for groups that finish early. ACE questions 12–14 are challenging extensions for students who show excellent spatial skills.

Summarize

The summary can be as simple as checking to be sure everyone agrees with the answers. Let a few students describe strategies they found useful for matching plans to buildings or vice versa.

Additional Answers

Answers to Problem 1.2

C.

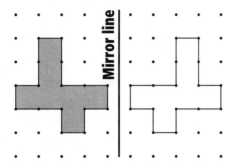

D.

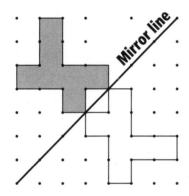

Answers to Problem 1.2 Follow-Up

2. There are a total of six mirror lines, one through each pair of opposite vertices and one through the midpoints of each pair of opposite sides.

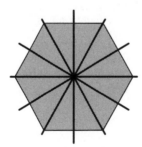

Answers to Problem 1.3

A.

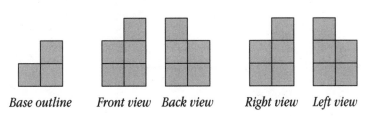

Base outline   *Front view*   *Back view*   *Right view*   *Left view*

B. Possible answer:

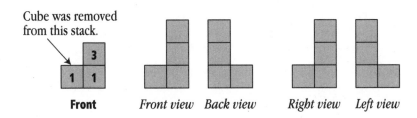

Cube was removed from this stack.

Front   *Front view*   *Back view*   *Right view*   *Left view*

C. Possible answer:

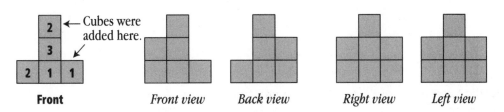

Cubes were added here.

Front   *Front view*   *Back view*   *Right view*   *Left view*

Answer to Problem 1.4 Follow-Up

The front of the building is the mirror image of the back. For example, if the front view has a stack of three cubes on the left, the back view will have a stack of three cubes on the right.

Answers to Problem 1.6 Follow-Up

3. No cubes can be removed.

4. No cubes can be removed.

For the Teacher: Extending Questions 3 and 4

In questions 3 and 4, some students may notice that, although no cubes can be *removed* from the building as it stands, the cubes could be *rearranged* to cut down on the number of cubes needed to construct a building in accordance with the building plans. The base plan on the left shows the cubes for building C rearranged. Like the original building, this new building matches set 4. The base plan on the right shows the cubes for building D rearranged. Like the original building, this new building matches set 2.

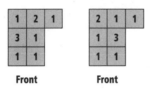

Front   Front

ACE Answers

Connections

9. For the building plans in question 1, base perimeter = 12 units, front perimeter = 10 units, and right perimeter = 10 units. For the building plans in question 3, base perimeter = 12 units, front perimeter = 12 units, and right perimeter = 12 units.

For the Teacher: Discussing Question 9

Question 9 is a good question to discuss as a class. Ask how the perimeter of the base compares to the perimeter of a rectangle that would enclose the base.

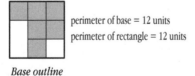

perimeter of base = 12 units
perimeter of rectangle = 12 units

Base outline

The perimeter of the base is the same as the perimeter of the framing rectangle. Can students speculate as to why this is true? Ask similar questions about the front and right views.

Mathematical Reflections

2. A figure has line symmetry if there is an imaginary line through the figure such that the parts of the figure on either side of the line are mirror images of one another. If you were to fold a figure along this *mirror line* (or *line of symmetry*), the part of the figure on one side of the line would match exactly the part on the other side.

For the Teacher: Mirror Lines

Each point of a figure on one side of a mirror line has an image point on the opposite side that is exactly the same distance from the mirror line and lies on a line through the original point perpendicular to the line of symmetry.

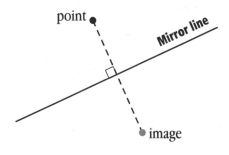

Making Buildings

This investigation challenges students to reason visually and analytically about cube buildings and to create cube buildings that fit given sets of plans. So far in this unit, students have made plans from buildings and have matched buildings to sets of plans. They have had opportunities to make cube buildings matching given views, but here they are challenged to construct buildings that fit complete sets of building plans and to consider whether there is more than one building that fits a given set of plans.

In Problem 2.1, Reconstructing Ruins, students make buildings from base plans and then solve mysteries about them. Problem 2.2, Constructing Buildings from Plans, challenges students to make cube buildings from sets of building plans and to compare their buildings with those of their classmates. Students begin to understand that a set of building plans may not determine a unique building. In Problem 2.3, Building from Incomplete Plans, students work with building plans that are missing one of the three diagrams—the base outline, the front view, or the right view. This problem also asks students to consider the greatest and least numbers of cubes needed to create a building with the given views.

Mathematical and Problem-Solving Goals

- **To develop efficient strategies for reading a set of building plans and for constructing a building that matches a given set of plans**

- **To reason visually and analytically about cube buildings**

- **To make observations about similarities and differences in the buildings that fit a given set of plans or incomplete set of plans**

Materials		
Problem	**For students**	**For the teacher**
All	Calculators, cubes (20 per student), building mat (made in Problem 1.1), grid paper (about 6 sheets per student), sugar cubes (optional; for homework)	Transparencies 2.1A to 2.3 (optional), cubes, transparent grid

Reconstructing Ruins

Launch

- Ask pairs to construct the buildings in parts A and B on separate building mats.

Explore

- Have pairs create a set of building plans for each of their buildings.

- Allow pairs to move to the follow-up when they are satisfied with their answers to the problem.

Summarize

- In a class discussion, ask pairs to share and discuss their reasoning for their answers to the questions in the problem and the follow-up.

Assignment Choices

ACE questions 1, 2, and unassigned choices from earlier problems

---

Making Buildings

In the last investigation, you learned how to draw plans for cube buildings. In this investigation, you will begin by solving mysteries about some ancient buildings. Then, you will construct buildings based on complete and incomplete sets of building plans. By comparing your buildings with those of your classmates, you will determine whether more than one building can be constructed from a set of plans.

2.1 Reconstructing Ruins

For an explorer like Emily Hawkins, carefully analyzing plans of ancient buildings is one way of learning about the culture of the people who once inhabited a city. In this problem, Emily is trying to answer some questions about two buildings that were discovered among the ruins of Montarek.

Did you know?

People lived in "modern" cities over 4000 years ago. In 1922, archaeologists discovered the ruins of the ancient city of Mohenjo-Daro in Pakistan. This city was laid out on a grid containing broad central boulevards with shops. In the city was a huge building where wheat and barley were stored. Some archaeologists believe this building was similar to a modern bank. Many of the estimated 40,000 residents of Mohenjo-Daro lived in private houses with indoor plumbing. This luxury was made possible by an extensive sewer system, which was maintained by public workers.

Tips for the Linguistically Diverse Classroom

Rebus Scenario The Rebus Scenario technique is described in detail in *Getting to Know Connected Mathematics*. This technique involves sketching rebuses on the chalkboard that correspond to key words in the story or information you present orally. Example: some key words and phrases for which you may need to draw rebuses while discussing the material on this page: *grid* (a grid), *shops* (simple rectangular buildings with symbols indicating a type of shop), *wheat* (wheat next to a loaf of bread), *bank* (rectangular building labeled with a dollar sign), *indoor plumbing* (a sink or a toilet).

Problem 2.1

In A and B, construct the building represented by the base plan. Then, make a set of building plans for each building on grid paper. Remember that a set of building plans consists of the base outline, the front view, and the right view.

A.

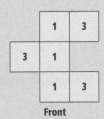

Front

B.

Front

C. Emily has studied some ancient writings she found among the ruins of Montarek. She thinks that one of the two buildings was used as a lookout post to watch for the approach of enemies or friendly travelers. Look at your building plans of the two buildings. Which do you think might have been used as a lookout post? Write at least two or three sentences to explain your answer.

D. Emily has discovered part of a diary kept by one of the residents of ancient Montarek. The diary indicates that the resident lived in the building from part A. Emily shows you a translated entry from the diary:

After dinner I went upstairs to my room. The stars were very bright, so I made my way to the tower from where I gazed at the stars. I can look down on the roof of my room from the tower, but I cannot see the tower from the windows of my room.

By examining your cube model from part A, the building plans you made for the building, and clues from the diary entry, identify which cube(s) on the building might have been the location of the resident's room. Write an explanation for your answer.

■ **Problem 2.1 Follow-Up**

Design a building and imagine that your room is in one of the cubes. Write a diary entry that could be used to figure out where your room is located.

Answers to Problem 2.1

A. See page 39e.   B. See page 39e.

C. Building B is the more likely lookout post because of its three towers.

D. Answers will vary. The room was most likely the top cube of the front left corner. The facts that the resident walked upstairs to the room and could see the roof of the room from the tower indicate that the room was the top cube of one of the two-cube sections. The fact that the resident could not see the tower from the room indicates that the room was most likely in the front left corner of the building.

Answer to Problem 2.1 Follow-Up

Answers will vary.

Constructing Buildings from Plans

**Grouping:
Individuals**

Launch

■ Introduce students to the six sets of plans for which they will construct buildings.

Explore

■ Circulate as students work, asking questions that raise the issue of whether a building is unique to a set of plans.

Summarize

■ Display students' base plans as they explain their solutions, and ask the class to verify that each solution works.

■ Return to the question of how many buildings fit a given set of plans, and allow students to discover the uniqueness problem of building plans: a set of plans does not necessarily specify a unique building.

Assignment Choices

ACE questions 7–10 and unassigned choices from earlier problems

2.2 Constructing Buildings from Plans

So far, you have been drawing sets of building plans by looking at cube models of buildings. Sometimes it is necessary to work the other way. In the next problem, you get to be the explorer and make cube models of buildings from sets of building plans.

Problem 2.2

Emily Hawkins uncovered six ancient stone tablets in her last expedition to the ruins of Montarek. A set of building plans is drawn on each tablet. The plans are shown below and on the next page. Use cubes to make a model of a building corresponding to each set of plans.

As you make each building, compare your models with those of other students in your class. Note how the other cube models are like yours and how they are different. Record a base plan for each building so that you can share what you did with the class.

Set A

Base outline

Front view

Right view

Set B

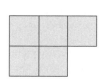

Base outline

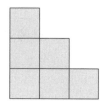

Front view

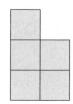

Right view

Answers to Problem 2.2

Positions shown in white are the same for each building that fits the building plans.

A.

Front

B.

1	2	1
3	1	

1	2	1
3	2	

2	2	1
3	2	

2	1	1
3	2	

2	2	1
3	1	

C–F.   See page 39e.

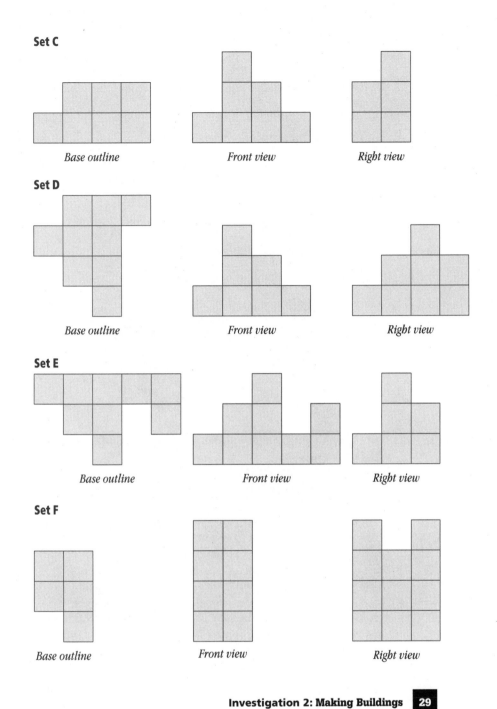

Set C

Base outline

Front view

Right view

Set D

Base outline

Front view

Right view

Set E

Base outline

Front view

Right view

Set F

Base outline

Front view

Right view

Answers to Problem 2.2 Follow-Up

1. Possible answer: For part A, everyone made the same building. For the other parts, some people made different buildings. For example, in part B, some people used two cubes in both the front center stack and the back center stack, and other people had two cubes in only one of these stacks.

2. Yes; Sometimes, cubes may be "hidden" so they do not appear in the front and right views. So, a building with these hidden cubes will have the same building plans as a building without them.

Building from Incomplete Plans

Launch

- Introduce students to the incomplete sets of plans for which they will make buildings and base plans.

Explore

- After students work individually on parts A–C, they may work with a partner on parts D and E.

- Assist students who are having trouble, and encourage others to think more creatively about the problem.

Summarize

- Review solutions to the problem, verifying that students see that many buildings may correspond to an incomplete set of plans.

- Designate a display area where students can add additional solutions as they find them over the next several days. (*optional*)

Assignment Choices

ACE questions 3–6, 11, 12, and unassigned choices from earlier problems

---

■ **Problem 2.2 Follow-Up**

1. Did you find any differences between the cube buildings you made from the building plans and the buildings others in your class made? If so, describe the differences.

2. Do you think that more than one building can be made from a set of building plans? Explain your answer.

2.3 Building from Incomplete Plans

Often Emily finds only partial sets of building plans. She uses these incomplete plans to construct *possible* buildings. In the next problem, you will be working from some of Emily's incomplete sets of building plans.

Did you know?

Architects often prepare blueprints of building plans. A *blueprint* is like a combination of a drawing and a photograph. An architect or builder draws his plans in pencil or India ink on special paper that lets light pass through. This drawing is placed on blueprint paper and exposed to strong light. Special chemicals on the blueprint paper react with the light and turn blue. Because the light does not pass through the lines drawn in pencil or ink, they stay white on the blueprint paper. Before the blueprint is used, it is washed in water to remove the chemicals. This ensures that the white lines do not turn blue when the blueprint is used in the light. Blueprints allow architects and builders to make hundreds of exact copies of building plans for clients and workers.

Answers to Problem 2.3

A. Possible answers: There are 57 buildings that fit this incomplete set of plans. Each building has a base plan with a 3 in the uppermost position and a 1 in the lowermost position. Here are two possible front views and corresponding base plans.

Front view

Front

Front view

Front

Problem 2.3

Emily discovered some pieces of pottery among the ruins of Montarek. Each piece of pottery has an incomplete set of building plans painted on it.

An incomplete set of plans is shown in A–C. In each case, one of the three diagrams is missing—either the base outline, the front view, or the right view. On grid paper, draw the missing view and a base plan for each building.

A.

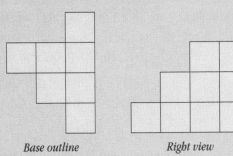

Base outline   *Right view*

B.

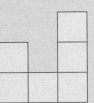

Base outline   *Front view*

C.

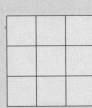
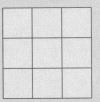

Front view   *Right view*

D. What is the greatest number of cubes you can use and still fit the plans given in part C? Make a base plan for a building with the greatest number of cubes.

E. What is the least number of cubes you can use and still fit the plans given in part C? Make a base plan for a building with the least number of cubes.

B. There are 55 buildings that fit this incomplete set of plans. Each building has a base plan with a 2 in the upper left position, a 1 in the top center position, and a 1 in the mid center position. Here are two possible right views and corresponding base plans.

Right view   **Front**   *Right view*   **Front**

C–E.   See page 39f.

■ **Problem 2.3 Follow-Up**

1. Which incomplete set of building plans was easiest to use to create a base plan? Why do you think this is so?

2. Which incomplete set of building plans was hardest to use to create a base plan? Why do you think this is so?

3. Do you think there is more than one base plan possible for a set of incomplete building plans? Why or why not?

4. Compare the base plans you made in part C of the problem with the base plans made by other students in your class. Are your base plans the same or different? Explain your thinking.

Answers to Problem 2.3 Follow-Up

1. Possible answer: Set B; Incomplete plans that include a base outline are easiest to use, because the base outline gives you a place to start.

2. Possible answer: Set C; Incomplete plans without a base are the most difficult to use, because you have to figure out how the two views fit together and determine what kind of base is possible.

3. Possible answer: Yes; in each part of the problem there were many possible base plans.

4. Possible answer: There were lots of different base plans. The only requirement is that a base plan fit inside a 3 by 3 grid. The largest base possible is 3 squares by 3 squares. The smallest base possible has only five squares.

As you work on these ACE questions, use your calculator whenever you need it.

Applications

1. Using your cubes, construct the building shown by this base plan:

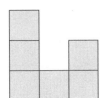

Front

a. Draw a set of building plans for the building on grid paper. Remember that a set of building plans includes the base outline, the front view, and the right view.

b. Modify your cube building to make a different building with the same building plans. Make the base plan for your new building.

c. Explain how your new building can have the same building plans as the original building even though it has a different base plan.

2. Record a base plan for this building:

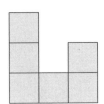

| Base outline | Front view | Right view |

Answers

Applications

1a. See below left.

1b. See below left.

1c. The base plans are different because the buildings are different. The building plans are the same because both buildings were built using these plans. The new building has the same base as the original, and it looks the same when viewed from the front and the right.

2.

Front

(**Teaching Tip:** The set of plans in question 2 determines a unique building. Discuss this with students, helping them to see that there is no way to "hide" cubes.)

1a.

Base outline   *Front view*   *Right view*

1b. Possible answers:

Front   Front   Front

3. See below right.

4–5. See page 39g.

In questions 3–5, an incomplete set of building plans is given. On grid paper, draw the missing part of the plans—front view, right view, or base outline—and record a base plan for your building.

3.

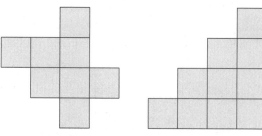

Base outline   *Right view*

4.

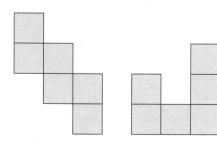

Base outline   *Front view*

5.

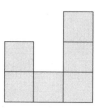

Front view   *Right view*

3. Many answers are possible. Here are two:

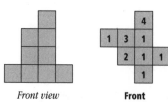

Front view   **Front**   *Front view*   **Front**

**Ruins of the Propylaea and the Temple of
Athena Nike (427–424 B.C.) in Athens, Greece**

6. Use your cubes to construct the building shown in this base plan:

3	1	1
1	1	2
1		

Front

   a. Draw a set of building plans for the building on grid paper.

   b. Remove two cubes from the building so that the front view is unchanged.
      Make a base plan of the new building.

   c. Rebuild the original building. Remove one cube so that the right view *and* the
      front view are unchanged. Make a base plan of the new building.

   d. Rebuild the original building. What is the greatest number of cubes you can
      remove so that the base outline is unchanged? Explain your answer, and make
      a base plan of the new building.

6a.

Base outline

Front view

Right view

6b. Possible answers:

3	1	1
	1	2

Front

3		
1	1	2
1		

Front

3	1	
1	1	2

Front

6c. Possible answers:

3	1	1
1		2
1		

Front

3		1
1	1	2
1		

Front

6d. See left.

6d. 3; You can remove the three cubes that are not part of the foundation.

1	1	1
1	1	1
1		

Front

Connections

7a. 3; Possible explanation: You can add the heights of the stacks and divide by the total number of stacks, or you can even out the stacks so they are the same height.

7b. no; The average height can be found by adding the numbers on the base plan and dividing by the number of squares.

7c. See page 39g.

7d. The average height of the building in question 2 is $\frac{10}{6} = 1.67$. This means that if we took all the cubes and put them evenly on the base—making each stack the same height— each stack would be 1.67 cubes high.

8.

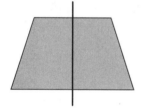

Connections

7. The *average height* of a cube building is the mean of the numbers of cubes that are stacked on each square of the building's base outline. Look at this base plan:

Front

a. Find the average height of this building. Explain how you found your answer.

b. Is it necessary to construct the building with cubes to find the average height? Why or why not?

c. If you multiply the average height of the building by the number of squares in the base outline, what is the result? Is anything special about this number?

d. Find the average height of the building shown in ACE question 2. What does your answer mean?

In 8–10, make a drawing that shows all lines of symmetry for the figure.

8.

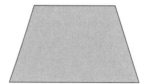

9.

10.

Extensions

11. Emily Hawkins has uncovered a stone tablet that describes an ancient building. Emily asks you to help her figure out what the building may have looked like. She shows you this passage, which has been translated from the writing on the tablet:

A building stands at the border of Montarek. The building is made from 12 cubic blocks of stone. Its foundation occupies a rectangular area of 6 square units. Two towers, each made from 4 cubic blocks of stone, reach into the air from opposite corners of the building.

a. Use cubes to make a model of what the building might have looked like. Assume that each face of a cube is 1 square unit of area. Make a base plan of your building, and describe how you figured out how to make your building.

b. Are you sure your building is exactly what the ancient building looked like, or are there other possibilities? Explain your answer.

Investigation 2: Making Buildings 37

---

9. There are no lines of symmetry for the parallelogram.

10.

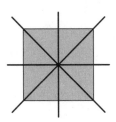

Extensions

11a. Possible answer: I first made a rectangle of 6 squares, then added the two towers, then counted the blocks and realized that the building had 12 blocks.

4	1	1
1	1	4

Front

11b. There are three possibilities for the building; here are the two others.

1	1	4
4	1	1

Front

Front

12. Answers will vary.

12. Design a building with no more than 15 cubes. Try to make your building a challenge. Draw a set of plans for your building, including a base outline, a front view, and a right view. Also make a base plan for your building. If there is more than one building that fits your plans, draw a base plan for at least one of these buildings.

Mathematical Reflections

In this investigation, you have learned to use building plans—the base outline, the front view, and the right view—to construct a cube model of a building. Sometimes you made a building from a complete set of plans; other times, one of the views was missing. When you constructed a building from a set of building plans, your building was sometimes different from the buildings made by other students. These questions will help you summarize what you have learned:

1 When you are building from an incomplete set of plans, which piece of information is the hardest to do without: the base outline, the front view, or the right view? Why?

2 If you are given the front view and the right view but not the base outline, how can you always figure out what is the largest possible base that will fit the two views? Explain. Use an example if it helps to explain your thinking.

3 Fatima thinks she has found a good way to build a cube building from a complete set of plans. She builds the base, the right side, and the front side separately and then tries to put them together. What do you think of her method? Will it always work? Why or why not?

Think about your answers to these questions, discuss your ideas with other students and your teacher, and then write a summary of your findings in your journal.

Tips for the Linguistically Diverse Classroom

Diagram Code The Diagram Code technique is described in detail in *Getting to Know Connected Mathematics*. Students use a minimal number of words and drawings, diagrams, or symbols to respond to questions that require writing. Example: Question 2—A student might answer this question by drawing a front view that is three cubes wide, labeled *3 cubes wide*, a right view that is four cubes wide, labeled *4 cubes wide*, and a 3 by 4 rectangle labeled *largest base = 3 × 4 rectangle*.

Possible Answers

1. It is usually hardest to do without the base outline, because it gives you a starting point for construction. If the base outline is missing, the number of possibilities may be quite large.

2. The largest base will be a rectangle with the width of the front view as one dimension and the width of the right view as the other dimension. For example, if the front view is three cubes wide and the right view is four cubes wide, the largest possible base is a 3 by 4 rectangle.

3. This is not a good way to try to construct a cube building, because putting the front view and right view on the base often creates problems. For example, for the building plans below, if you build the front view on the front of the base, you will not be able to build a right view that fits the set of plans.

Base outline

Front view

Right view

TEACHING THE INVESTIGATION

2.1 • Reconstructing Ruins

Problem 2.1 expands the investigation by having students consider the practicality of possible buildings as fortresses. By imagining a bird's eye view they can decide which would be more effectively defended.

Launch

Refer students to Problem 2.1 in their books, or display Transparency 2.1. Divide students into pairs.

> Work with your partner to construct the buildings shown in parts A and B. Make each building on a separate building mat.

Check each pair's buildings to verify that they are correct.

> Now, work with your partner to make a set of building plans for each of your buildings. When you finish, work on parts C and D.

Explore

As you visit pairs working, look for misunderstandings and for good strategies for thinking about each part of the problem. When students move to parts C and D, remind them to discuss their answers with their partner.

> You are asked to write explanations for your answers. If you and your partner don't agree, be sure to explain carefully what each of you thinks and figure out where you disagree. When you are satisfied with your answers to Problem 2.1, move to the follow-up.

Assign ACE question 11 as an extra challenge for pairs that finish early.

Summarize

Allow several pairs to read their explanations for the decisions they made. Students might argue for either of the buildings in part C. Some may reason that the three-cube tower in building A would allow guards to see in all directions. Others may argue with this, saying that the side of the building opposite the tower would be vulnerable to attack; the two-cube section would prevent guards from seeing close to the building and from fighting off attacks from that side. Most students will argue that building B is the better lookout post. The three towers would give guards unrestricted views in all directions and allow them to better defend the building during attack.

For part D, most students will argue that, since the resident went *upstairs* after dinner and looked *down* from the tower to the roof of his or her room, the room must have been on the second floor. The entry also indicates that the tower could not be seen from the resident's room. Of the cubes in the second story, the one in the front left corner is the one from which it would be least possible to see the tower. Some students will argue that the resident could lean out the window and see the tower from any of the second-floor cube rooms. This may be the case, but is less likely for the front left cube.

2.2 • Constructing Buildings from Plans

You may find that some students will be able to draw a base plan for a building that fits a set of plans without physically constructing the building from cubes. Although these students' analytic skills are developing nicely, they need to work on their visualization skills as well. Encourage them to take the time to make the cube building and to practice visually checking a solid object against written plans.

Launch

Introduce the story of the six sets of building plans found by Emily Hawkins.

> Today you get your first chance to be a full-fledged cube-building constructor. Your challenge is to build a cube building that matches each set of plans. You will record each of your buildings by making a base plan.

Remind students that a base plan looks like a base outline with numbers in the squares indicating how many cubes are in each stack.

Have students first work individually and then check their answers with their partner's.

Explore

As you circulate, ask questions about the students' buildings.

> Is this the only building that will fit this set of plans?
>
> Is there any part of this building that must be the same for *all* buildings that fit this set of plans?
>
> Is there a position in which you have a choice about whether or not to add a cube?

Some students will use naive strategies to produce a building that matches a set of plans. For example, some may build one-cube-thick front views and one-cube-thick right views and then try to slide them together. Encourage these students to first build the base and then go back and forth between the two views to place the remaining cubes. Similarly, concentrating on only one view may result in difficulties. The two views together describe a three-dimensional building; each view alone gives only two-dimensional information.

Summarize

One way to start the summary is by giving groups of four students transparencies on which to record all the solutions they found for each part of the problem.

Display some of their base plans at the overhead. Have students explain why they believe their answers are correct; this will give you a good indication of how facile they are at reading building plans. Ask the class to verify whether the buildings represented by the base plans fit the sets of building plans. Students who are having difficulty may be helped by this dialogue.

The question of how many buildings fit a given set of plans should arise in the discussion. Return to the issue of what all the buildings that fit a given set of plans have in common.

Which stacks must be the same in each building? Which stacks can vary?

For example, only one building fits set A.

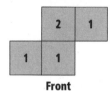

Front

However, for set B, there are five possibilities, which have from 8 to 10 cubes.

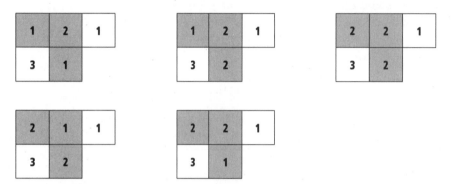

For two positions (shown in white), the number of cubes is the same for each building. The remaining three positions may have one or two cubes, but at least one of the two positions to the left of the fixed 1 must have two cubes, and at least one of the middle two positions must have two cubes.

For most of the sets of plans, more than one building is possible. As students compare their base plans with those of other students, they will grasp for themselves the idea that different buildings can sometimes be built from the same set of plans.

2.3 • Building from Incomplete Plans

In this problem, students work with incomplete sets of building plans. In the process they explore what each diagram of a building plan contributes to the specification of a building and draw conclusions about which diagram is hardest to do without.

Launch

In this problem students focus on the different buildings they can make from a given incomplete set of plans and determine the greatest and least numbers of cubes that will fit a given set of plans.

> In her work, Emily often uncovers only part of a set of building plans. She has to reconstruct what a building may have looked like by using only two parts of a set of plans.

In this problem, you are given incomplete plans for three buildings. One diagram—the base outline, the front view, or the right view—is missing from each set. Your task is to make a cube building that fits the diagrams. Then, you need to draw the missing diagram and make a base plan for your building.

Work by yourself to construct your buildings and to make your drawings. When you are finished, collaborate with your partner on parts D and E. Later, you will have a chance to see what the rest of the class found. You may want to revise your answers then.

Explore

Encourage students to be creative in parts A and B. Instead of just building the base and then adding a minimal number of cubes to match the other given view, ask them to search for more interesting variations. If time permits, encourage students to come up with multiple buildings of their own.

Some students will have a hard time with part C because no base is given to get them started. You may need to focus them on what they can determine about the base from the two given views.

How wide is the base? How long is the base from the side?

Challenge students who finish early to move on to the follow-up. These questions foreshadow the uniqueness discussion that will occur in Investigation 3.

Summarize

Review students' responses to the problem, then discuss the follow-up questions. In the summary, confirm that students recognize that many buildings sometimes correspond to an incomplete set of building plans.

One good way to summarize is to work as a class to record several buildings that fit the incomplete plans in parts A or B. In evaluating a partial set of plans, students should first identify positions that must have the same number of cubes for all buildings that will fit the plans. If students are interested, you may want to start a display area for them to add additional solutions as they are discovered, perhaps over the next several days.

For part C, ask students to identify the largest possible base (this is a rectangle with the width of the front view as one dimension and the width of the right view as the other—in this case, a 3 by 3 square). Then discuss parts D and E, which ask for the greatest and least numbers of cubes that can be used to make a building that fits the incomplete plans in part C.

Additional Answers

Answers to Problem 2.1

A.

Base outline   Front view   Right view

B.

Base outline   Front view   Right view

Answers to Problem 2.2

The notation 1/2 means that either 1 or 2 cubes can be placed in the position.

C.

3	1	1
1	1	2	1

3	2	1
1	1	2	1

3	2	1
1	2	1	1

3	2	1
1	2	2	1

3	1	1
1	2	2	1

D.

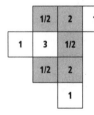

E.

F.

 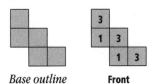

Answers to Problem 2.3

C. There are numerous possible buildings. Here are two possible base outlines with corresponding base plans.

Base outline   **Front**   *Base outline*   **Front**

D. The building with the greatest number of cubes is a 3 by 3 by 3 cube. It requires 27 cubes.

Front

E. A building with the least possible number of cubes is shown below. It requires 11 cubes.

Front

For the Teacher: Clarifying Problem 2.3 Part C

The "building" with base plan below has 9 cubes and matches the plans from part C. However, in this unit we require that each cube in the base touch at least one other cube face to face.

Front

ACE Answers

Applications

4. Many answers are possible. Here are two:

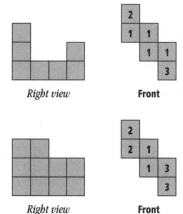

Right view   **Front**

Right view   **Front**

5. Many answers are possible. Here are two:

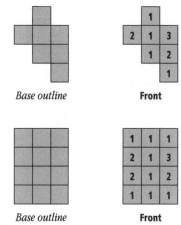

Base outline   **Front**

Base outline   **Front**

Connections

7c. The result is the total number of cubes in the building. This is because the average height is the total number of cubes divided by the number of squares in the base outline. If you multiply the average height by the number of squares, you are finding

$$\frac{\text{total number of cubes}}{\text{number of squares in base outline}} \times \text{number of squares in base outline}$$

which is the same as

$$\text{total number of cubes} \times \frac{\text{number of squares in base outline}}{\text{number of squares in base outline}}$$

which is just the total number of cubes times 1.

INVESTIGATION 3

Describing Unique Buildings

In Investigation 2, students learned that a set of building plans does not always specify a unique building. That investigation foreshadowed this one by asking questions about the least and greatest numbers of cubes that could be used to fit a set of plans. Students instinctively think that if we specify that the least number of cubes be used—that is, that a *minimal building* be built—only one building will be possible from a set of plans. They also instinctively think that if we specify that the greatest number of cubes be used—that is, that a *maximal building* be built—several buildings may be possible. In this investigation, they discover that the reverse is true: there may be several minimal buildings that fit a set of plans, but there is only one maximal building. Thus, a set of building plans, along with the constraint that the largest possible number of cubes be used, defines a unique building.

In Problem 3.1, Finding All the Possibilities, students construct every building that fits a given set of plans. In the follow-up they discover that the maximal building is unique while the minimal building is not. In Problem 3.2, Finding Maximal and Minimal Buildings, students build the maximal building and a minimal building for each of three sets of building plans. In Problem 3.3, Unraveling an Ancient Mystery, they construct a maximal building based on plans found in ancient Montarek and then speculate about what the building may have been used for.

Mathematical and Problem-Solving Goals

- *To become proficient at reading a set of plans and constructing a building that matches a set of plans*

- *To reason visually and analytically about cube buildings*

- *To understand that several minimal buildings may fit a set of plans, but only one maximal building*

- *To develop a recording scheme to keep track of all buildings that fit a set of plans*

Materials		
Problem	**For students**	**For the teacher**
All	Calculators, cubes (20 per student), building mat (made in Problem 1.1), grid paper, sugar cubes (optional; for homework)	Transparencies 3.1 to 3.3 (optional), cubes, transparent grid
3.1	Labsheet 3.1 (1 per group)	

Finding All the Possibilities

At a Glance

Grouping: Small Groups

Launch

- Have students each construct a building to fit the plans and then confer with their groups.

- As a class, inspect the various base plans that were found.

Explore

- As groups record the base plans for all the buildings they can find, suggest ways they can generate more buildings.

- Challenge students to make buildings by using the greatest or least number of cubes possible.

Summarize

- At the overhead, record all the base plans students have found, and help them conduct a systematic search to ensure they have found all possibilities.

- Discuss patterns in the collection of base plans, and talk about minimal and maximal buildings.

Describing Unique Buildings

In the last investigation, you found that it is sometimes possible to construct more than one building from a set of building plans. We need a way to interpret building plans so that they specify only one building. That way, if you and a friend work independently but use the same set of building plans as a guide, you will construct identical buildings.

3.1 Finding All the Possibilities

In this problem, you will work with your group to find all the buildings that fit a set of building plans.

Problem 3.1

With your cubes, make a building that corresponds to this set of building plans:

Base outline   *Front view*   *Right view*

A. Draw the base plan of your building. Compare your base plan with the base plans made by other students in your group.

B. How many different buildings can be made from this set of building plans? Work with your group until you are sure you have found all of the different buildings. Draw a base plan for each building.

Assignment Choices

ACE questions 5, 6, and unassigned choices from earlier problems

Answers to Problem 3.1

See page 51e.

Problem 3.1 Follow-Up

1. Of the different base plans you made in Problem 3.1, are there any squares with numbers that do not change? If so, identify the squares with numbers that always remain the same.
2. Look carefully at the base plans for the different buildings you found in Problem 3.1.
   a. What is the least number of cubes used for any of the buildings?
   b. How many different buildings can be made from the least number of cubes?
   c. What is the greatest number of cubes used for any of the buildings?
   d. How many buildings can be made from the greatest number of cubes?

3.2 Finding Maximal and Minimal Buildings

Emily Hawkins has translated some interesting facts about the way buildings were constructed in ancient Montarek. For a set of building plans, buildings made using the *least* number of cubes are called **minimal buildings**. Buildings made with the *greatest* number of cubes are called **maximal buildings**.

In Problem 3.1, you discovered that the *maximal building is unique* and *the minimal building is not necessarily unique*. This means that only one maximal building can be made from a set of building plans. However, using the same plans, it may be possible to construct more than one minimal building.

Investigation 3: Describing Unique Buildings   **41**

Launch

- Review what students have learned about minimal and maximal buildings.
- Discuss the idea that adding the constraint that a set of plans describes a *maximal* building also specifies a *unique* building.

Explore

- Have students construct minimal and maximal buildings individually and then check answers in their groups.
- For groups who are ready, challenge them to find all the minimal buildings, or all the possible buildings, for a given set of plans.

Summarize

- Share answers to the problem in a class discussion.
- Record all the minimal buildings students have found for a set of plans, and help them search for any they have missed. (*optional*)

Answers to Problem 3.1 Follow-Up

1. Three squares have the same number in every base plan:

Front

2. See page 51e.

Assignment Choices

ACE questions 1–4 and unassigned choices from earlier problems

Problem 3.2

The plans in A–C were discovered by Emily among the ruins of Montarek. For each set of plans, find a minimal building and the maximal building. Record the base plans for your minimal building and the maximal building on grid paper. For each part, compare your minimal and maximal base plans with those of others in your class or group.

A.

Base outline   *Front view*   *Right view*

B.

Base outline   *Front view*   *Right view*

C.

Base outline   *Front view*   *Right view*

■ Problem 3.2 Follow-Up

Create a set of building plans for which the minimal building is the same as the maximal building.

Answers to Problem 3.2

See page 51f.

Answers to Problem 3.2 Follow-Up

Possible answer:

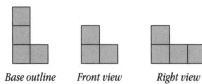

Base outline   *Front view*   *Right view*

Unraveling an Ancient Mystery

Unraveling an Ancient Mystery

Emily Hawkins' explorations of the ruins of Montarek have helped her to make an important discovery! She discovered that when making a building from a set of building plans, the people of Montarek always constructed the maximal building. Emily feels that this discovery can be useful in solving another ancient mystery about the ruins of Montarek.

In her explorations, Emily came across the following set of building plans for a large and mysterious ancient building:

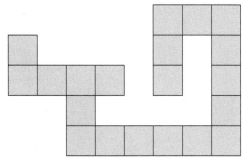

Base outline

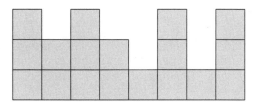

Front view

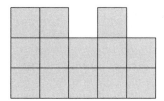

Right view

Investigation 3: Describing Unique Buildings **43**

At a Glance

Grouping:
Small Groups

Launch

■ Review Emily's discovery that all buildings in Montarek were maximal buildings.

Explore

■ Have groups construct minimal and maximal buildings for the set of plans, make base plans of their buildings, then move to the follow-up.

■ For groups who are ready, challenge them to find other minimal buildings that fit the plans.

Summarize

■ Share answers to the problem in a class discussion.

■ Investigate which squares in the base plan are the same for every minimal building. (*optional*)

Assignment Choices

ACE questions 7, 8, 9–11 (as an extra challenge), and unassigned choices from earlier problems

Assessment

It is appropriate to use Check-Up 1 after this problem.

Problem 3.3

A. Work with your group to construct a minimal building from the set of building plans. Make a base plan of your building on grid paper.

B. Work with your group to construct the maximal building from the set of building plans. Make a base plan of your building on grid paper.

■ **Problem 3.3 Follow-Up**

Recall that the people of Montarek always constructed maximal buildings. How might the people of Montarek have used this ancient building? Explain your reasoning.

Answers to Problem 3.3

See page 51f.

Answer to Problem 3.3 Follow-Up

Answers will vary. Students may think in modern terms and say that it looks like a shopping mall. Others might try to place it in its historical perspective and say it could be a castle or some other fortified area, as there are lookout towers in several locations.

Applications • Connections • Extensions

As you work on these ACE questions, use your calculator whenever you need it.

Applications

1. Look carefully at this set of building plans:

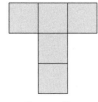 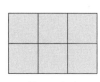

Base outline   *Front view*   *Right view*

a. Construct a minimal building from the building plans. Make a base plan of the building.

b. Suppose it costs $5 to put a special glaze on the top of each exposed cube in a building. How much would it cost to put the glaze on the exposed top of your minimal building?

c. Now construct the maximal building from the building plans. Make a base plan of the building.

d. How much will it cost to glaze the exposed top of the maximal building?

e. How do the costs of glazing the roofs of the minimal and maximal buildings compare? Will the relationship between the cost of glazing the roof of a minimal building and the cost of glazing the roof of a maximal building always be the same as what you found here? Why or why not?

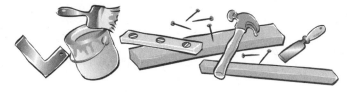

Investigation 3: Describing Unique Buildings **45**

Applications

1a.
```
2  1  2
   2
   1
```

1b. 5 cubes × $5 = $25

1c.
```
2  2  2
   2
   1
```

1d. 5 cubes × $5 = $25

1e. The costs will always be the same because the top is the same as the base, which is the same whether the building is minimal or maximal.

2. Each minimal building has 15 cubes. The maximal building has 19 cubes. Possible answer:

Minimal building

	1		
1	1	3	2
1	2	1	
	2	1	

Maximal building

	1		
2	2	3	2
1	2	2	
	2	2	

3. Each minimal building has 16 cubes. The maximal building has 20 cubes.

Minimal building

	1	1	1
1	1	1	3
		2	1
	2	1	

Maximal building

	1	1	1
1	2	2	3
		2	2
	2	2	

Connections

4a. Answers will vary.

4b. The answer depends on the building, but it can be no less than 12.

In 2 and 3, make base plans for a minimal building and the maximal building with the given set of building plans. Tell how many cubes are needed for each building.

2.

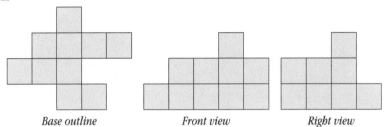

Base outline   *Front view*   *Right view*

3.

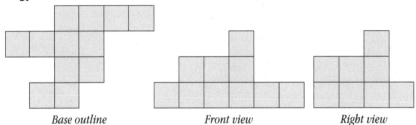

Base outline   *Front view*   *Right view*

Connections

4. Use your cubes to construct a maximal building that has a roof area of 12 square units.

    a. On grid paper, make a base plan of your maximal building, and draw a set of building plans for it.

    b. How many cubes did you use to construct your building?

5. Construct a building with 10 cubes.

   a. On grid paper, make a base plan for your building, and draw a set of building plans for it.

   b. Do you think your building is a minimal building, the maximal building, or neither? Explain your reasoning.

6. Here is a set of incomplete plans for a building.

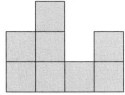
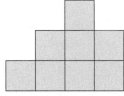

Base outline   *Front view*

   a. Build every possible building that will fit these plans. Make base plans to record each possible building.

   b. Explain how you know you have found every possible building.

Extensions

7. Emily Hawkins has uncovered another mystery among the ruins of Montarek. She is trying to reconstruct an ancient building that has completely disappeared—no trace of it remains. One of the clues that Emily has is that the building was a maximal building made from 13 cubes. Emily also has a piece of ancient parchment that shows the front view of the building:

Front view

5a. Answers will vary.

5b. Answers will vary.

6a. See page 51g.

6b. Possible answer: I am sure I found them all because I fixed some spaces and systematically varied the other spaces. For example, the space at the top of the second column must be 2 or 1. First I listed all the base plans with a 2 in this space, then I listed all the base plans with a 1 in this space.

Extensions

7a. Possible answer:

7b. Here are the building plans for the building in part a:

Base outline

Front view

Right view

7c. The building I drew is only one possibility. There are several possible bases, but I had to keep in mind that I only had 13 cubes to work with.

8a. See below right.

8b. The number of sides is the same as the number of lines of symmetry, so a regular polygon with 20 sides will have 20 lines of symmetry.

8c. 101

a. Using your cubes, construct a building that fits the clues. Draw a base plan of the building on grid paper.

b. Make a set of building plans for your building.

c. Do you think the building you have constructed is a model of the same building that once existed in Montarek, or do you think there are other possibilities? Explain your reasoning.

8. a. For each of the regular polygons shown below, find the number of lines of symmetry. Organize your data into a table.

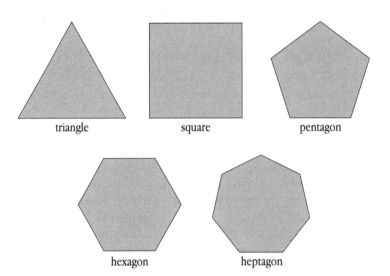

triangle   square   pentagon

hexagon   heptagon

b. Find a pattern in your data that will help you predict how many lines of symmetry a regular polygon with 20 sides will have. Describe your method of predicting.

c. How many lines of symmetry will a regular polygon with 101 sides have?

8a.

Sides	3	4	5	6	7
Lines of symmetry	3	4	5	6	7

hexagon   triangle   square   pentagon   heptagon

In 9 and 10, a set of plans for a building is given. The buildings are unusual in that some of the cubes on certain levels fit on half of a cube in the level below. This means that if you look at the building from the top, what you see is not a picture of the base outline. For each building, try to construct the maximal building that fits the plans. Find a way to record your building on paper.

9.

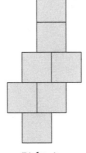

Base outline   Front view   Right view

10.

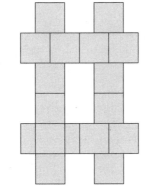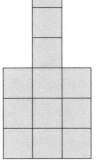

Base outline   Front view   Right view

9. Possible answer: The diagram below shows an outline of each layer of the building. An x in a layer matches up with the x in the layer below.

x
layer 1

x
layer 2

x
layer 3

x
layer 4

x
layer 5

10. See below left.

10. Possible answer: The diagram below shows an outline of each layer of the building. An x or y in a layer matches up with the x or y in the layer below.

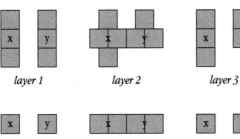

x   y
layer 1

x   y
layer 2

x   y
layer 3

x   y
layer 4

x   y
layer 5

x   y
layer 6

11. There are many possible answers; one is shown below. Positions shown in white have fixed numbers for every possible building.

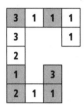

11. Use exactly 20 cubes to make a model from the building plans below. Record a base plan for your building.

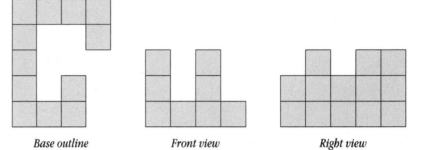

Base outline   *Front view*   *Right view*

Mathematical Reflections

In this investigation, you have built models to consider what additional constraint, or requirement, can be added to a set of building plans so it will specify only one building. These questions will help you summarize what you have learned:

1 Is it possible to build several buildings that fit a set of plans made up of a base outline, a front view, and a right view? Explain and illustrate your answer.

2 Is it possible for there to be a set of plans with the three views—base outline, front view, and right view—that has only one possible building? If so, how is this building different from the example you gave in question 1?

3 What can you require that will make every set of plans specify only one building? Explain why this requirement will give a unique building.

Think about your answers to these questions, discuss your ideas with other students and your teacher, and then write a summary of your findings in your journal.

Possible Answers

1. Yes, it is possible for several buildings to fit a set of plans. There may be places where cubes can be "hidden" so that they are not seen in the views given in a set of plans. Here is a set of plans that corresponds to more than one building:

Base outline

Front view

Right view

2. See below left.

3. If we require that the building be a maximal building, the building will be unique.

2. Yes, some building plans correspond to a unique building. Here is a set of plans that corresponds to only one building:

Base outline   *Front view*   *Right view*

TEACHING THE INVESTIGATION

3.1 • Finding All the Possibilities

Students have seen that several different buildings may fit a set of plans. Help students begin to find a systematic way of finding all the possible buildings for a given set of plans. The questions here are challenging, but can be fun and exciting for students.

Launch

Refer students to Problem 3.1 in their books, or display Transparency 3.1.

> I would like each of you to construct a building that fits this set of plans. When everyone in your group has finished, look at each other's buildings and check to see whether they fit the plans.

Give students a few minutes to construct their buildings and to work with their groups to check them. Then, bring the class together again.

> Are there different buildings that fit this plan?
>
> How are all the buildings that fit this plan alike? How are they different?

Students will probably mention that the buildings use different numbers of cubes. Give each group a copy of Labsheet 3.1.

> You will now work with your group to try to find all the buildings that can be assembled from this set of plans.

Labsheet 3.1 contains several copies of the base outline for the building. Explain that students will record their base plans by writing numbers in the squares.

> Start by making base plans for the buildings your group has found so far. Then, look for more buildings that fit the plans. Try to organize your work and be systematic about your search.

Tell students that later the class will collect all the base plans that have been found and examine the buildings that are particularly interesting.

Explore

As you observe and assist the groups, you might suggest that one strategy for generating additional buildings is to start with a building that fits the plans and then try to add or remove cubes so that the resulting building still matches the plans.

As groups get involved in the problem, you can raise the issue of trying to use the least or greatest number of cubes possible to make a building that fits the plans.

Summarize

As a class, record the base plans students have found on a transparency of Labsheet 3.1. Either record the plans as students call out their answers, or have students come to the overhead and reproduce their plans. Keep track to be sure all 17 base plans are found. If students have not discovered them all, ask questions that focus on conducting a systematic search.

> Do we have all the possibilities with a 3 in the upper left corner?

When all 17 base plans have been recorded, help students examine the collection for patterns.

> Let's look for patterns in our base plans. Do any squares have the same number on all of the base plans? Why does this make sense?

There are three stacks that must be one cube high:

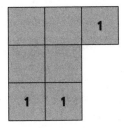

Discuss the follow-up questions. Question 2 asks about maximal and minimal buildings.

> What is the least number of cubes anyone used to create a building that fits the plans? (*11*) We call a building made with the least possible number of cubes a *minimal building*.

> What is the greatest number of cubes that anyone used? (*15*) We call a building made with the greatest possible number of cubes a *maximal building*.

> How many different buildings have 11 cubes? (*2*) How many different buildings have 15 cubes? (*1*)

> Is there another maximal building that fits the plans, but that is different from the one we found?

Let students present their answers and their reasons. They will probably see that the answer is no. If not, propose the following argument. Suppose we have two different buildings that we think are maximal. Since the buildings are different, there must be a place where one of the buildings has a cube and the other doesn't. If we add a cube to the building that does not have a cube in that place, it must still fit the plans. Therefore, the building was not maximal to begin with.

3.2 • Finding Maximal and Minimal Buildings

Students may have been puzzled that a single building plan could result in more than one "correct" building. Now they will be able to see see a way to obtain a unique result by adding a new condition—a constraint.

Launch

Remind students of what they discovered in Problem 3.1 about minimal and maximal buildings.

> In the last problem, you found that for a set of building plans, there may be more than one minimal building, but there is only one maximal building. This means that if we add the constraint that the building must be maximal, anyone using a given set of building plans will make the same building.
>
> In this problem, you will build minimal and maximal buildings for three sets of plans.

Explain that students will work individually to construct their buildings and then in their groups to compare and check their answers.

Explore

As students work, keep an eye out for those who are ready for an extra challenge. Ask such groups to find all the minimal buildings for each of the plans or to find every possible building that fits one of the sets of plans.

Have students who finish early work on the follow-up.

Summarize

In a class discussion, allow students to present their answers. After a student gives an answer, ask whether everyone agrees and whether anyone found something different.

Help students summarize what they have learned about maximal and minimal buildings. If you have time, display a transparency with base outlines for the plans in part A, and record all the minimal buildings students found. Then, as a class, search for any minimal buildings they have missed. This provides excellent practice in combinatorial reasoning in a visual context. You can do this with the other sets of plans as well.

Unraveling an Ancient Mystery

With the realization that a maximal building is unique, students can apply this finding to the building plan at Montarek.

Launch

Review Emily's discovery that the people of Montarek always built maximal buildings. Then, refer students to the problem, or display Transparency 3.3.

> Emily discovered this set of building plans for a large and mysterious ancient building. In your groups, you will build a minimal building that fits these plans, and then you will make a base plan of your minimal building. You will need to pool your cubes so that you have enough.

> Then, add cubes to your minimal building until you have a maximal building, and make a base plan of your maximal building.

Explore

When a group has finished the problem, have them consider the follow-up question, which asks what the (maximal) building may have been used for.

If any groups need an extra challenge, ask them to find other minimal buildings that fit the plans. There are many! You could designate a bulletin board where students can display the minimal buildings they find over the next few days.

Summarize

Have groups share their answers, and resolve any differences. You might ask how they worked together on the problem.

> How did you divide up the work in your group so that each person could contribute?

You could ask which squares in the base plan have the same number for every minimal building. Since there are so many minimal buildings, the class may find that their ideas about which numbers are fixed change as they discover more minimal buildings. Ten positions have the same number of cubes for every minimal building:

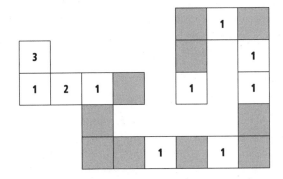

Additional Answers

Answers to Problem 3.1

A. Possible answers:

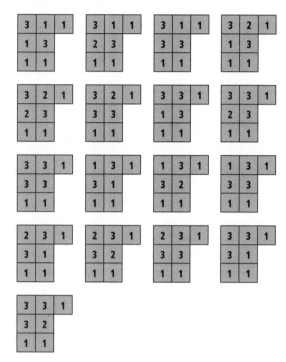

B. 17 buildings are possible.

Answers to Problem 3.1 Follow-Up

2. a. 11

    b. Two buildings can be made from 11 cubes.

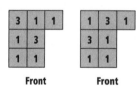

    c. 15

    d. One building can be made from 15 cubes.

Front

Answers to Problem 3.2

A.

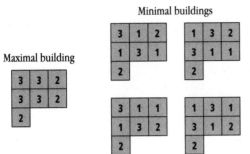

B.

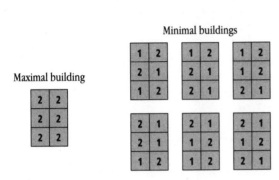

C.

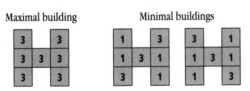

Answers to Problem 3.3

A. There are many possibilities, each with 31 cubes. Possible answer:

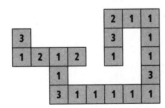

B. The maximal building has 45 cubes.

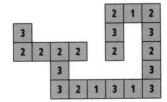

ACE Answers

Connections

6a. There are 21 possible buildings. Positions that are fixed for all buildings are shown in white.

Isometric Dot Paper Representations

So far in this unit, students have used sets of building plans—the right view, the front view, and the base outline—to read and record information about buildings. Each view in a set of plans shows the building from directly in front of a side. This investigation introduces a new way to represent a building. An *isometric* representation shows a building as viewed from a corner, so that three of its sides are seen in one drawing. Students will use isometric dot paper as a tool for creating such representations.

Problem 4.1, Drawing a Cube, introduces students to isometric dot paper and asks them to make isometric drawings of a cube. In Problem 4.2, Drawing a Cube Model, students draw a stack of three cubes in every possible way on isometric dot paper. They use 2-D isometric models of cubes as design tools to help them visualize the isometric views. In Problem 4.3, Drawing More Complex Buildings, they add a cube to their stack to make an L shape and then draw all the possible views. Since the L is not symmetrical, there are more views of it than of the three-cube stack. In Problem 4.4, Creating Your Own Building, students design their own buildings and represent them on isometric dot paper. They then consider whether a diagram on isometric dot paper represents a unique building.

Mathematical and Problem-Solving Goals

- **To understand how the dots are arranged on isometric dot paper and how this arrangement allows cube buildings to be drawn from corners**

- **To visualize the relationship between the angles of an actual cube and an isometric drawing of a cube**

- **To copy existing figures onto isometric dot paper**

- **To construct buildings that fit isometric drawings and make isometric drawings of cube buildings**

- **To use 2-D isometric models of cubes as design tools**

- **To develop strategies for reading an isometric drawing and constructing a building that matches the drawing**

- **To observe similarities and differences in building produced to fit isometric drawings**

Materials		
Problem	**For students**	**For the teacher**
All	Calculators, cubes (20 per student), building mat, isometric dot paper, sugar cubes (optional; for homework)	Transparencies 4.1 to 4.4 (optional), transparent isometric dot paper
4.1	Angle rulers and scissors, envelope (1 per student)	
4.2	Labsheet 4.2 (1 per student)	

Isometric Dot Paper Representations

In the last investigation, you learned how a set of building plans represents a unique maximal building. You also found that a set of building plans may correspond to several different minimal buildings.

In this investigation, you will learn about another way to represent three-dimensional cube buildings on paper. You will learn how to look at a cube building from a corner and make a drawing that shows three of its faces.

The Flat Iron building in New York City has an interesting corner.

You have used grid paper and dot paper in your mathematics classes to help you make graphs, record rectangles, and find areas. In this investigation, you will use a new kind of dot paper that will help you make drawings of the way buildings look from their corners. This new paper is called *isometric dot paper.* The word *isometric* comes from the Greek language and has two parts: "iso" meaning "the same," and "metric" meaning "measure." So isometric means "same measure."

4.1 Drawing a Cube

Below is part of a sheet of isometric dot paper. Take a few minutes to study the paper. Why do you think it is called isometric dot paper?

Think about this!

- Describe the pattern of dots on isometric dot paper. How is it different from the pattern on the usual kind of dot paper?

- Focus on a dot and the six dots that are its "nearest neighbors." You may want to mark your center and the six surrounding dots so that you can find them easily. Find the number of degrees in each of the angles that you can form with any three of the dots that you marked (one of the dots must serve as the vertex of the angle).

- What are the side lengths of the smallest equilateral triangle you can make by connecting three dots?

- What other patterns do you see in the way the dots are arranged or in the measures of angles on isometric dot paper?

Investigation 4: Isometric Dot Paper Representations **53**

Drawing a Cube

At a Glance

**Grouping:
Individuals or Pairs**

Launch

- Allow students to explore making drawings on isometric dot paper.

- As a class, discuss how isometric dot paper differs from other dot paper.

Explore

- Have students individually make a drawing of a cube on isometric dot paper.

- Challenge students who finish to draw the opposite view of the cube.

Summarize

- Display the two views of a cube, and ask students to share their strategies for drawing the cube.

- Discuss the follow-up, which explores the issue of how the angles on an actual cube compare to the angles in an isometric drawing of a cube.

Assignment Choices

Drawing a Cube Model

At a Glance

Grouping: Individuals

Launch

- Have each student cut out the set of 2-D models from Labsheet 4.2.

- Explain that students will be making isometric views of a three-long.

Explore

- As students make their drawings, help those who are having trouble.

- As you circulate, make sure students are not drawing illegal or extraneous lines.

Summarize

- As a class, discuss all the views that were drawn, summarizing them at the overhead and making sure all six were found.

- Have students describe their strategies for drawing the views.

Problem 4.1

Hold a cube level with your eyes. Look at the cube carefully. Turn it to see each of its corners. Tip the cube so that you see the corner nearest you in the center with six vertices evenly spaced around this center corner. Your challenge is to find a way to draw the cube in exactly this position on a sheet of isometric dot paper.

When you and your partner have each successfully drawn the cube, try to find a way to show a different view of the cube in a picture on the dot paper. The two pictures should look quite different. One should show the top of the cube and one should show the bottom.

■ Problem 4.1 Follow-Up

What is the measure of each angle of the cube drawn on dot paper? How do these measures compare to the measures on the real cube?

4.2 Drawing a Cube Model

Some people find it very hard to visualize cube models as they are pictured on isometric dot paper. To help you investigate drawing cube models on isometric dot paper, cut out the 2-D models of cubes on Labsheet 4.2. Store the models in an envelope so you don't lose them.

These models are like the drawing you made on isometric dot paper. If you turn a 2-D model upside down, you should see the drawing you made of the bottom of a cube. You can use the models to help you in Problem 4.2. Notice how the 2-D model can be placed to fit the dots on the isometric dot paper.

 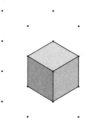

Assignment Choices

ACE questions 1–4 and unassigned choices from earlier problems

Answer to Problem 4.1

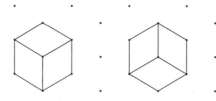

Answer to Problem 4.1 Follow-Up

The cube drawn on dot paper has angle measures of 60° and 120°. On the actual cube, all angles measure 90°.

Problem 4.2

Make a stack using three cubes. Hold the stack in the air and turn it, observing it from many different views.

  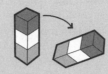

Your challenge is to find every way this stack of three cubes can be pictured on isometric dot paper.

You can use your 2-D cube models to help you draw your pictures. Be sure you stack the models in the same way that the real cubes are stacked. You can place the 2-D models on the dot paper so you can better see where to draw the lines.

Talk to your partner and check each other's work so that you can both get better at drawing models of cube arrangements on isometric dot paper.

■ **Problem 4.2 Follow-Up**

Describe any patterns you see in the isometric drawings of the stack of three cubes.

Answer to Problem 4.2

See page 61i.

Answer to Problem 4.2 Follow-Up

Possible answer: The three-longs can be drawn by starting with the two views of a single cube. Two views are oriented vertically, two slant to the right, and two slant to the left.

Drawing More Complex Buildings

Grouping: Individuals

Launch

- Explain that students will be drawing isometric views of a letter L, created by adding a cube to a three-long.

- Ask the class how many views they think can be made of the L shape.

Explore

- As students make their drawings, help those who are having trouble, and suggest that they use their 2-D models to help visualize the drawings.

Summarize

- At the end of the period, ask students what they have discovered so far about drawing the L shape.

- Allow students to continue drawing views of the L as homework.

Assignment Choices

Ask students to continue investigating the possible views of the L shape.

4.3 Drawing More Complex Buildings

Now that you have an idea of how to draw stacks of cubes and how to use your 2-D cube models to help you make drawings, you can try your skills on more complicated arrangements of cubes. In this problem, you will make drawings of cube buildings made from four cubes.

> **Problem 4.3**
>
> **A.** Use four cubes to make the building shown below. On isometric dot paper, make as many drawings of this cube building, turned in the air in different ways, as you can.
>
>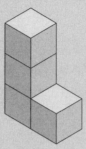
>
> **B.** Explain why you think you have found all possible ways to draw the building on isometric dot paper.

■ **Problem 4.3 Follow-Up**

Now, make a different arrangement with four cubes. On dot paper, draw as many pictures as you can of your cube arrangement turned in different ways. Remember that the 2-D cube models can help you figure out what lines to connect on the dot paper.

Answer to Problem 4.3

A. See page 61j.

B. Possible answer: I took each view of a three-long and found all the different ways I could add a cube to make an L. For each of the 6 views of a three-long, there are 8 places where I can add a cube, so there are 6 × 8 = 48 possible views.

Answer to Problem 4.3 Follow-Up

See page 61j.

Now it is your turn to be the architect. As you make drawings of your own building, think about what information someone else will be able to tell about your building from your drawings.

Problem 4.4

A. On your building mat, create a building using at least 7 cubes but no more than 12 cubes. Make a drawing of it on isometric dot paper. Label the drawing to indicate which corner the building is being viewed from (front right, right back, back left, or left front).

B. Now turn the building and make a drawing from the opposite corner. Label the view to indicate the corner.

C. If you give a friend just these two drawings, do you think he or she will be able to construct the building exactly as you have made it? Explain.

D. Exchange the isometric dot paper drawings that you made with the drawings that your partner made. Construct a cube building from your partner's drawings.

E. Were you able to get enough information from the drawings to re-create the building your partner constructed? Explain why or why not.

F. Was your partner able to re-create your building from your drawings? Why or why not?

G. In the last investigation, you found that a set of building plans does not always allow you to construct a unique building. However, if you specify that the building must be maximal, it will be unique. Do you think a set of two diagrams on isometric dot paper corresponds to a unique building? Or, is it possible that more than one building can be made from a set of two diagrams on isometric dot paper?

■ **Problem 4.4 Follow-Up**

Would a set of diagrams showing all four corners of a building determine a unique building? Explain your reasoning.

At a Glance

***Grouping:
Individuals***

Launch

■ Introduce the design problem to the class, making sure everyone understands what is to be done.

Explore

■ Remind students that they can use their 2-D design cubes if needed.

■ For students ready for an extra challenge, suggest they construct other shapes and draw all the isometric views possible.

Summarize

■ Ask students to share their buildings and drawings with the class.

■ Discuss the problem of uniqueness—that isometric views do not necessarily specify a unique object.

Answers to Problem 4.4

Answers will vary.

Answer to Problem 4.4 Follow-Up

Even a set of drawings showing all four corners will not necessarily show all the cubes that might be in a building.

Assignment Choices

ACE questions 5–7 and unassigned choices from earlier problems

Answers

Applications

1.

2.

3.

4.

As you work on these ACE questions, use your calculator whenever you need it.

Applications

In 1–4, a view is shown from the front right corner of a building.

* Copy each building, exactly as it appears, on isometric dot paper.

* Make a cube model of the building. Then, make a drawing from the back left corner of the building.

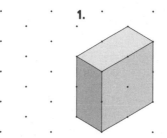

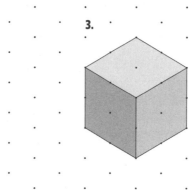

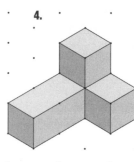

Connections

5. a. Use cubes to construct a model of each building in questions 1–4. For each building, draw a set of building plans on a sheet of grid paper.

b. Is there more than one building that will fit the building plans you have made? Why or why not?

Extensions

6. How many cubes touch the orange cube face to face?

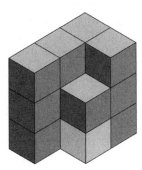

Connections

5a. See page 61k.

5b. Only one building will fit the plans for the buildings in questions 1, 2, and 4. More than one building fits the set of plans for the building in question 3, but there is only one building that fits the isometric drawing.

Extensions

6. 3

7. 60

7. How many cubes are needed to build this rectangular solid?

Mathematical Reflections

In this investigation, you used isometric dot paper to learn a new way to make representations, or drawings, of cube buildings. These questions will help you summarize what you have learned:

1 Explain, in your own words, how isometric dot paper is arranged so that it is possible to draw cube buildings from the corners.

2 **a.** What are the measures of the angles formed by the edges of a face of a *real* cube?

   b. On isometric dot paper, what are the measures of the angles formed by the edges of a cube?

   c. Explain any differences or similarities in the measures you found.

3 Imagine that your friend gives you isometric drawings from all four corners of a cube building. Will you be able to read enough information to construct a building exactly like the original? Why or why not?

Think about your answers to these questions, discuss your ideas with other students and your teacher, and then write a summary of your findings in your journal.

Possible Answers

1. When you look at cubes from perspectives other than straight on, the angles at the corners do not appear to be 90°. On isometric dot paper, the dots are arranged to make it easy to draw angles of 60° and 120°. This allows you to draw views that match what your eye sees when you look at a cube from a corner.

2a. All the angles measure 90°.

2b. The angles measure 60° and 120°.

2c. In both the cube and the drawing, opposite angles are equal and all angle measures for a face add to 360°. For the cube, all angles are equal. For the drawing, opposite angles are equal but adjacent angles are not equal.

3. Even in drawings of all four corners, a cube can still be hidden, or there may not be a cube there at all. For example, these two buildings have the same four isometric drawings.

2	2	2
2	1	2
2	2	2

Front

2	2	2
2		2
2	2	2

Front

Tips for the Linguistically Diverse Classroom

Original Rebus The Original Rebus technique is described in detail in *Getting to Know Connected Mathematics*. Students make a copy of the text before it is discussed. During discussion, they generate their own rebuses for words they do not understand as the words are made comprehensible through pictures, objects, or demonstrations. Example: Question 2a—key words for which students may make rebuses are *measures* (a degree symbol), *angles* (three different angles), *edges* (a cube with an arrow pointing to an edge), *cube* (a cube).

TEACHING THE INVESTIGATION

4.1 • Drawing a Cube

The ability to draw a cube in perspective may be a real breakthrough for some students. Encourage them to look at photos and identify right angles—which may not look like right angles from their point of view.

Launch

Give each student a sheet of isometric dot paper, and allow students a few minutes to explore making drawings on the paper. You might have them refer to the "Think about this!" in the student edition to guide their exploration. Here are answers to the questions in the "Think about this!" feature:

- On rectangular dot paper, the dots form vertical and horizontal lines. On isometric dot paper, they form slanted lines as well.

- Angles with measures 30°, 60°, 120°, and 180° can be formed by these dots.

- The smallest equilateral triangle has sides of length 1 centimeter.

- Six equilateral triangles can be formed around each point by connecting the point to neighboring points. Triangles, parallelograms, and rhombuses can also be formed by connecting points. Students may see other patterns as well.

Bring the class together to launch the problem.

> Look carefully at the isometric dot paper. Do you see anything special or different about the arrangement of dots on this paper compared to other dot paper you have used?
>
> Use a pencil to darken a single point on your dot paper. Now draw line segments to connect the dot you selected to the dots that are its nearest neighbors.

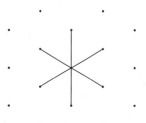

When students have had a minute, demonstrate at the overhead.

> What do you notice about the line segments you have drawn? (*They are all the same length.*)
>
> This kind of dot paper is called *isometric dot paper.* The prefix *iso-* means "equal" and *metric* means "measure." So, *isometric* means "equal measure."

On isometric dot paper, the points surrounding a dot are an equal distance from the dot. Is this true on regular dot paper? (*No. On regular dot paper, the dots on the diagonal are further away from a dot than the dots directly above, below, and to the right and left.*)

Hold a cube level with your eyes. Look at it carefully, turning it to see each of its corners. Tip the cube so that you see a corner with six surrounding corners evenly spaced around the center corner. Your challenge is to draw this view of the cube on isometric dot paper.

Students can work in pairs to help each other draw the cubes, but each student should make his or her own drawings.

Explore

When a student has successfully drawn a cube with the top showing, challenge him or her to tip the cube so that the bottom shows and to draw this view.

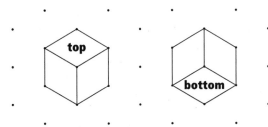

Summarize

Show the two views on the board or overhead, and ask students to describe their strategy for drawing the figures. Here are some strategies students have used:

■ Sam drew a hexagon and then "Y-ed it." To make the cube with the top showing, he drew a right-side-up Y. To make the cube with the bottom showing, he drew an upside-down Y.

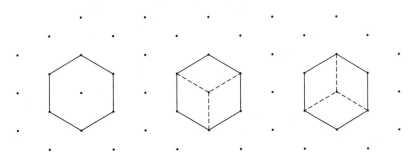

■ Elida started by drawing a sideways diamond. To make the cube with the top showing, she drew three vertical legs extending down from the diamond and then connected the ends of the legs.

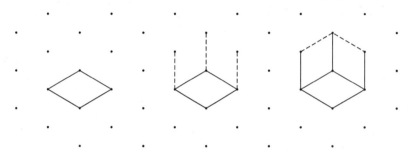

To make the cube with the bottom showing, she drew the legs sticking up from the diamond.

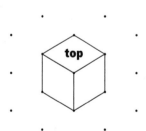

■ Noah traced the cube edges with his finger, drawing them on dot paper as he traced them.

Hold your cube so it looks like this picture. (*Point to the drawing showing the top of the cube.*)

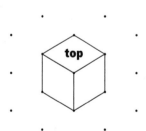

Assist students who are having difficulty. Sometimes having them close one eye will help.

How are the faces of the actual cube shaped? (*They are all squares.*) What shape is the top of the cube in the isometric drawing? (*a diamond or rhombus*) Are all the faces of the cube the same in the isometric drawing? (*yes*)

Now, discuss the follow-up questions.

Measure the angles of a cube face on the dot paper drawing. What are the measures? (*There are two 60° angles and two 120° angles.*)

How do the angles in an isometric drawing of a cube face compare to the angles in a face of an actual cube? (*The sum of the four angles in the drawing is the same as for the actual cube, 360°, but the sizes of the angles are different. All four angles in a face of an actual cube measure 90°.*)

4.2 • Drawing a Cube Model

In this problem, students use 2-D models of cubes as design tools to help them visualize cube buildings drawn on isometric dot paper and to draw isometric views of cube buildings.

Launch

Before you begin, have each student cut out the 2-D models from Labsheet 4.2. Give each student an envelope or bag in which to store the models.

In the last problem, you experimented with drawing a single cube on isometric dot paper. You found that you can draw two isometric views of a cube, one showing the top of the cube and one showing the bottom.

Make a stack of three cubes, and show it to the class.

I am going to call this stack of cubes a "three-long."

Make a three-long from your cubes. Now, turn it freely and look for views that can be drawn on isometric dot paper. Your challenge is to find every different view that can be shown on isometric dot paper.

Students should work in pairs, but each student should make his or her own set of drawings.

Explore

Some students will see how to get started right away; others will need to work harder to see as the dot paper sees. Circulate as students work, helping those who are having trouble.

Remind students that they can use their 2-D models to help them see where to draw lines. They can place the models on the dot paper and overlap them as needed to form the views of the three-long.

Check drawings carefully to see that students are not adding "illegal" lines. The only lines that they should draw are from a point to its nearest neighbor. The drawing below, for example, is not allowed because the dots connected to form the top and bottom of the box are not joined to their nearest neighbors.

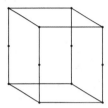

Students should also avoid drawing extraneous "legal" lines, as such lines can make seeing the cubes on dot paper very difficult.

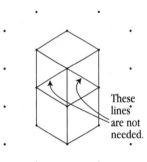

These lines are not needed.

You might suggest that students who are having trouble draw a single cube in either position (with the top or bottom showing) and then try to add cubes to the drawing to make a three-long.

Summarize

Select a student to show a view he or she found, then ask whether anyone found a different view. Continue until all six views have been shown. Summarize these views at the overhead.

Have students describe their strategies for seeing and drawing the views. You may want to demonstrate how the views can be drawn by starting with the views of a single cube.

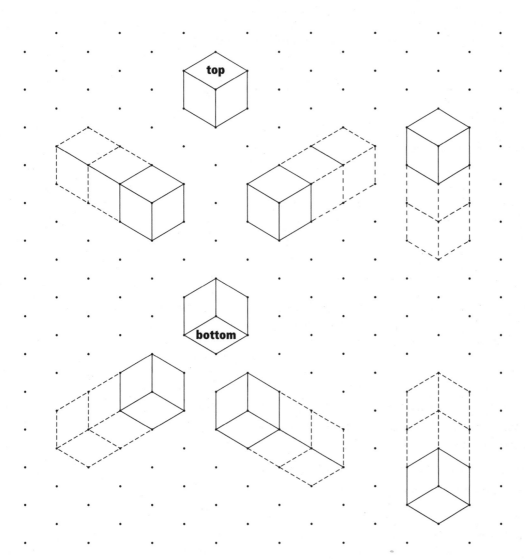

4.3 • Drawing More Complex Buildings

Students' work so far has shown them that isometric dot paper can be used to capture views of cubes and simple cube buildings. In this problem, another cube is added to a three-long to produce a more complex building. The problem develops both visual and spatial skills and visual reasoning.

Launch

> So far we have found that there are only two isometric views of a single cube, and six views of a stack of three cubes. Today we will add one more cube to our stack and see what happens to the number of possible views.

As you demonstrate, have each student make a three-long and then add one cube to a face to form a solid letter L.

Let's make a drawing of this L shape sitting up so that anyone can see that it is an L.

On a sheet of transparent isometric dot paper, draw an L like the one shown in the student edition.

How many different isometric views do you think will be possible if we allow the L to turn freely in space?

Take a few conjectures, and then let students work in pairs or small groups to make their drawings. Students should make their own drawings and then compare them with those made by others in their group.

Explore

Circulate, helping students who are having trouble getting started. Some students will struggle to draw even a few L shapes; suggest that they use their 2-D design cubes to help see the views. Others will begin to see families of L's associated with a particular view of a three-long.

Summarize

At the end of the class period, ask students what they know so far about the L-shaped figure and its representations on isometric dot paper. Students should begin to recognize that only certain positions of the L can be captured on isometric dot paper.

Since there are 48 possible views, it is unlikely that any group will have found them all. Have students continue working on the problem as homework.

At the beginning of the next class period, review what students discovered while doing their homework. Some may have drawn several views and then reasoned that 48 are possible. Some may have drawn all 48 views in a systematic way. Some may have drawn several views without discovering a systematic method for finding all the views. It is all right if students do not find all the views. All students will have success drawing some views and will be amazed at how many more views are made possible just by adding a single cube to the three-long.

4.4 • Creating Your Own Building

In this problem, students will design their own buildings, make isometric drawings from two of the buildings' corners, and exchange drawings with a partner. The buildings will stay firmly planted on their building mats, so students won't have to visualize them turning in space.

Launch

Remember that when we worked with building plans, sometimes more than one building could be made from a set of plans. To make sure there was only one building possible, we had to add the constraint that the building be a maximal building.

As part of this problem, you will investigate whether a set of drawings on isometric dot paper corresponds to a unique building.

Read, or have a student read, the entire problem out loud to the class. Make sure students understand what they are expected to do. Remind them that they can use their 2-D design cubes to help with their drawings, and that they can turn their building mats to look at their buildings from all four corners.

Explore

Circulate as students work. For those having difficulty representing their buildings on paper, suggest that they look at a corner and build the view of the corner with their 2-D design cubes. Then they can copy their isometric design onto dot paper.

Be prepared to offer an extra challenge to students with excellent visualization skills. You may want to have them create other simple shapes—such as a five-cube cross or a Z—and explore how many isometric drawings can be made of them.

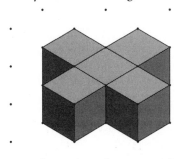
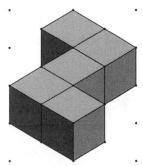

The cross is so symmetrical that only six views are possible—one for each position of a three-long. The Z will produce 24 views—four for each view of a three-long. Students can reason about this by looking at a three-long in one of its isometric positions and asking in how many ways the extra cubes can be added to form the Z. There are four positions in which the two additional cubes can be added to a three-long to produce a different view.

Summarize

Have some students share their buildings and drawings. You may want to display a few on the bulletin board.

Talk about the question of uniqueness. Since isometric drawings can hide cubes, a set of drawings does not necessarily correspond to a unique building. To help students see this, have them create the following buildings on their building mats.

2	2	2
2	1	2
2	2	2

Front

2	2	2
2		2
2	2	2

Front

Now, ask them to draw an isometric drawing of each building from a corner.

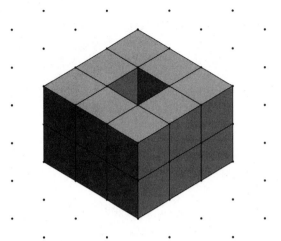

The corner views of the two buildings are the same. You cannot determine from the isometric view whether there is a cube in the center of the bottom layer.

Additional Answers

Answers to Problem 4.2

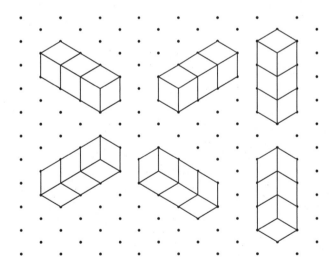

Answers to Problem 4.3

A. There are 48 different views that can be drawn on isometric dot paper. Here are a few:

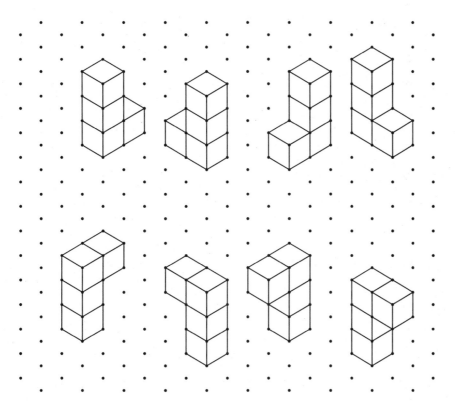

Answers to Problem 4.3 Follow-Up

Here are some other possible shapes made from four cubes:

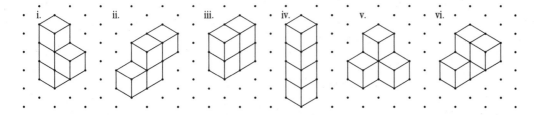

For shape i, we can add a cube on each of the four exposed faces of the center cube of a three-long. Since there are six possible views of a three-long, this gives 24 possible views. For shape ii, there are four ways to add two cubes onto opposite sides of a two-long to make an S shape, so there are 24 possible views. For shape iii, since there is only one view for each of the six positions of a two-long, there are only 6 possible views. Shape iv is similar to a three-long or a two-long; there are only 6 possible views. For shapes v and vi, because they are built on two-longs, there are six possible views of each.

ACE Answers

Connections

5a. for question 1:

Base outline   Front view   Right view

for question 2:

Base outline Front view   Right view

for question 3:

Base outline Front view   Right view

for question 4:

Base outline Front view   Right view

Ziggurats

This investigation introduces a special type of building called a ziggurat. *Ziggurats* are terraced pyramids in which each story is smaller than the one below it. Ziggurats served as temple towers for the ancient Assyrians and Babylonians.

The problems in this investigation give students more practice seeing, drawing, reasoning about, and building cube structures. In Problem 5.1, Building Ziggurats, students build a ziggurat from an isometric drawing and make a base plan and set of building plans for the ziggurat. In Problem 5.2, Representing Ziggurats, they build two ziggurats from base plans, and then draw a set of building plans for one ziggurat and an isometric drawing of the other.

Mathematical and Problem-Solving Goals

- **To become more proficient at designing cube buildings and drawing isometric views**

- **To reason visually and analytically about cube buildings drawn on isometric dot paper**

- **To relate isometric drawings of buildings to sets of building plans**

- **To use patterns to reason about the number of cubes needed to build a given building**

Materials		
Problem	**For students**	**For the teacher**
All	Calculators, cubes (20 per student), building mat, isometric dot paper, sugar cubes (optional; for homework)	Transparencies 5.1 and 5.2 (optional), cubes, transparent isometric dot paper

Student Pages 62–71   **Teaching the Investigation 71a–71e**

5.1

Building Ziggurats

At a Glance

Grouping:
Small Groups

Launch

- Have students build models of two ziggurats from their base plans.

- Discuss the elements of a ziggurat.

Explore

- Allow students to finish working on the problem and then consider the follow-up questions.

- Look for clever ways that students are thinking about follow-up question 2.

Summarize

- In a class discussion, allow students to present and explain their building plans.

- Discuss the number patterns present in a ziggurat.

Ziggurats

In this unit, you have learned three different ways to represent cube buildings with drawings. You can draw a *base plan* to record a building you have made; then, a friend can use your base plan to construct a replica of your building. You have also learned to make *a set of building plans*, which includes the base outline, the front view, and the right view of a building. Finally, you have learned to represent a building with an *isometric dot paper drawing*, which shows three sides of the building at once. In this investigation, you will use what you have learned to explore a special kind of pyramid that Emily Hawkins discovered among the ancient ruins of Montarek.

5.1 Building Ziggurats

Emily Hawkins found several pyramids among the ruins. She made a sketch of one of the pyramids using isometric dot paper.

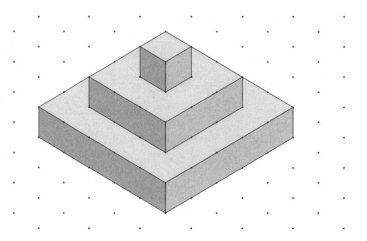

Notice that the pyramid has a square layer for each of its stories and that each layer is smaller than the layer beneath it. This kind of pyramid is called a *ziggurat* (pronounced *zig´-gu-rat*). Look up the word in your dictionary.

Assignment Choices

ACE question 1 and unassigned choices from earlier problems

Answers to Problem 5.1

A.

1	1	1	1	1
1	2	2	2	1
1	2	3	2	1
1	2	2	2	1
1	1	1	1	1

Front

B. See page 71c.

C. Answers will vary.

Did you know?

Archaelogists have uncovered over 30 ziggurats, some dating back to 3000 B.C., at sites in every important ancient Mesopotamian city. Ziggurats were built through great communal efforts as artificial mountains to house their local gods. Most of the ziggurats contained from three to seven levels. Sometimes the walls were painted different colors and plants and trees were grown on the terraces. This five-layer ziggurat built in the 13th century B.C. in the city of Tchoga Zanbil had a base of 350 square feet and was 174 feet high.

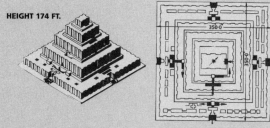

HEIGHT 174 FT.

Used with permission from the British Architectural Library, RIBA, London.

Problem 5.1

A. Make the base plan for the ziggurat shown on page 62.

B. Working with a partner, build the ziggurat with cubes, and make a set of building plans for it.

C. Why do you suppose people from ancient Montarek would build such pyramids? Explain your thoughts.

▇ Problem 5.1 Follow-Up

1. List the numbers of cubes in each layer of the ziggurat from the top layer to the bottom layer. Is there a pattern in this sequence? Explain your answer.

2. If the ziggurat in Problem 5.1 had a fourth and fifth layer of cubes added to the bottom, how many cubes would be needed for each of these new layers? Explain your reasoning.

Answers to Problem 5.1 Follow-Up

1. 1, 9, 25; These are the squares of the first three odd numbers.

2. You can continue the sequence above; 49 cubes would be needed for the fourth layer, and 81 cubes would be needed for the fifth layer.

Representing Ziggurats

Launch

- Explain Emily's discovery—that the people of Montarek built ziggurats with layers of more than one story.

Explore

- Allow groups to collaborate to construct the buildings, then have students make their representations individually.

- As you circulate, ask questions that focus students on the pros and cons of each type of representation.

Summarize

- In a class discussion, allow students to share their ideas about the advantages and disadvantages of each type of representation.

- Make sure each representation is analyzed thoroughly.

Assignment Choices

ACE questions 2–4, 7–8, and unassigned choices from earlier problems

---

5.2 Representing Ziggurats

Emily Hawkins found that the ziggurat pyramids of Montarek were not all the same size. Some were small; others were quite huge. She has uncovered different base plans of two ziggurats.

> **Problem 5.2**
>
> Below are sketches of base plans that Emily Hawkins found in the diary of an architect who was a citizen of ancient Montarek.
>
> | 1 | 1 | 1 |
> |---|---|---|
> | 1 | 2 | 1 |
> | 1 | 1 | 1 |
>
> **Front**
>
> | 3 | 3 | 3 | 3 | 3 |
> |---|---|---|---|---|
> | 3 | 5 | 5 | 5 | 3 |
> | 3 | 5 | 6 | 5 | 3 |
> | 3 | 5 | 5 | 5 | 3 |
> | 3 | 3 | 3 | 3 | 3 |
>
> **Front**
>
> **A.** Construct a model of the first ziggurat from cubes. Then, use your model to sketch a set of building plans for the ziggurat on grid paper.
>
> **B.** Use cubes to construct a model of the second ziggurat. Make a sketch of the ziggurat on isometric dot paper. Look back at the ziggurat from Problem 5.1 if you are unsure of how to begin.
>
> **C.** Compare the representations you have made of the two ziggurats. Write a short paragraph explaining to Emily which of the three representations—the cube model, the building plans, or the sketch on isometric dot paper—is the most useful for describing a ziggurat.

▇ Problem 5.2 Follow-Up

Design a ziggurat in which each layer is more than one cube thick. Draw a base plan for your ziggurat.

Answers to Problem 5.2

A–B. See page 71d.

C. Possible answer: Each of the representations has some good features. However, the cube model and the isometric drawing seem best to me because you can "see" the building. Since it is hard to carry around a cube model, the isometric drawing is better for showing someone the ziggurat. The building plans are easier to make and carry enough information to construct a cube model. So all three are useful, but I like the isometric drawing.

Answer to Problem 5.2 Follow-Up

See page 71d.

Applications • Connections • Extensions

As you work on these ACE questions, use your calculator whenever you need it.

Applications

1. Some of the buildings in Montarek are shaped something like a ziggurat, but not exactly. Here is a sketch from the front right corner of an ancient Montarek building:

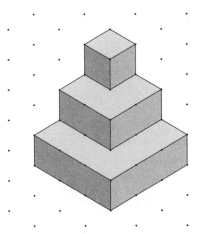

a. Make a cube model of the building and draw a base plan of your model on grid paper.

b. Make a set of building plans for the building on grid paper.

c. Make an isometric drawing of the building from the corner opposite the one above.

d. How would you describe the building? Write a brief paragraph that explains how the building is different from a ziggurat and how it is similar to a ziggurat. Also describe what you think the building might have been used for.

Answers

Applications

1a.

Front

1b.

Base outline

Front view

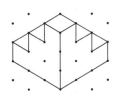

Right view

1c.

1d. Answers will vary.

2. e

3. a

4. d

2. Which of the following is *not* a corner view of the building represented by the base plan?

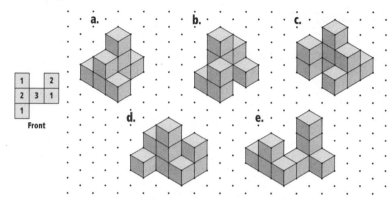

3. Which drawing below shows the building represented in the base plan viewed from the *front left* corner?

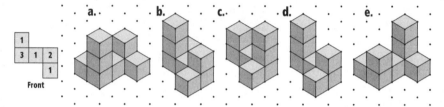

4. The drawing on the left shows one view of a building. Find another view of the building.

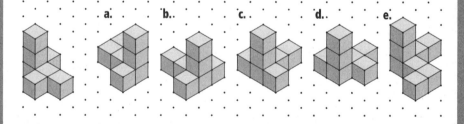

Connections

5. Choose a building in your community. Make a sketch of the building on isometric dot paper. When you are finished with your sketch, answer the following questions:

a. Is it possible to copy the building exactly on isometric dot paper? Explain how you made your sketch, including any assumptions or simplifications you made.

b. You will have to guess, but try to build a cube model that looks like a good representation of the building. (If it has a slanted roof, make a model without the roof.) Make a set of building plans for the building.

Houston, Texas

Connections

5. Answers will vary.

(**Teaching Tip:** This question is an opportunity for students to apply what they have learned about representing buildings to a building in their community. As students work on the project, encourage them to visualize the building they choose as being made out of cubes.)

Extensions

6a. See below right.

6b. Possible answers:

Front

Front

The building looks the same as the original building from the front right corner because the cubes in the back left corner are hidden.

Extensions

6. Emily Hawkins discovered the remains of an interesting building among the ruins of ancient Montarek. Below is a base plan of the building:

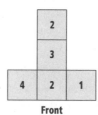

Front

a. Make a cube model of the building. Then, on isometric dot paper, make sketches of the building as it is viewed from each corner—the front right corner, the right back corner, the back left corner, and the left front corner. Label each sketch.

b. On grid paper, make a base plan that is different from the one above, but that represents a building that looks the same as the original when sketched from the front right corner. Explain why the building made from your new base plan would look the same as the original building on dot paper.

The ruins of the Incan city of Machu-Picchu in Peru

6a.

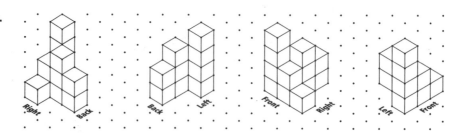

7. Using four cubes, make a figure in the shape of a cross. Imagine that the figure can turn in any direction in space, including upside down. Find *every* different way this figure can be drawn on isometric dot paper. Explain why you think you have found all the possible views. Two are shown here as examples:

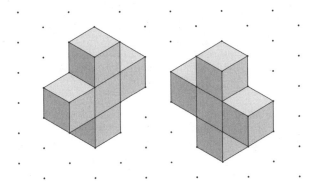

8. Make a T-shaped figure from five cubes. Imagine that the figure can turn in any direction in space. Find *every* different way this figure can be drawn on isometric dot paper. Explain why you think you have found all the possible views.

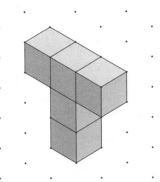

7. For each of the 6 views of a three-long, there are 2 ways to add 2 cubes to make a cross. This makes 12 views, but each view occurs twice since a cross is made up of 2 three-longs. Thus, there are 6 different views in all.

8. For each of the 6 views of a three-long, there are 4 ways to add 2 cubes to make a T, so there are 24 different views in all.

9a. Different volumes are possible, because cubes may be hidden from view.

i.   4 cubes

ii.   6 cubes, 7 cubes, or 8 cubes

iii. 5 cubes

iv.   This building could have anywhere from 27 to 42 cubes. The smallest building is a 3 by 3 by 3 cube. There could be up to 15 cubes hidden behind this cube. Below are base plans for the buildings with the smallest and largest volumes.

3	3	3
3	3	3
3	3	3

Front

1	1	1		
1	2	2	2	
1	2	3	3	3
	2	3	3	3
		3	3	3

Front

9b.

i.   10 units

ii.   8 units or 10 units

iii. 8 units

iv.   12 units, 14 units, 16 units, 18 units, 20 units, 22 units, or 24 units

---

9. Look carefully at each of the following building diagrams:

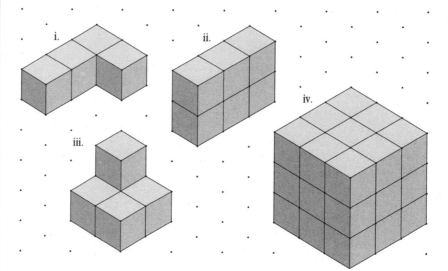

The *volume* of a cube building is a measure of how many *cubic units* it takes to *fill* the building. In other words, the number of cubes needed to make a cube model of a building is the volume of the building.

a. Without making cube models, find the volume of each building above—record how many cubes it would take to construct each of the buildings. If there are different numbers of cubes that could be used to construct a building, list all the possibilities, and explain why the different volumes are possible.

b. Without making cube models, record the perimeter of the base of each of the buildings. As in part a, if there is more than one perimeter possible for a building, list all the possibilities.

Mathematical Reflections

In this investigation you have sketched and examined special kinds of pyramids called ziggurats. These questions will help you summarize what you have learned:

1. Describe a ziggurat.

2. If a cube model of a ziggurat has five layers, each one cube thick, and the top layer is a single cube, how many cubes will it take to make the model? Explain why you think you are correct.

Think about your answers to these questions, discuss your ideas with other students and your teacher, and then write a summary of your findings in your journal. Be sure to include sketches if you think they would help your comments make more sense.

Possible Answers

1. A ziggurat is a building made of square layers. Each layer is a smaller square than the layer below it, giving the building a pyramid shape.

2. It will take 1 + 9 + 25 + 49 + 81 = 165 cubes. I think I am correct because the layers are square arrangements of cubes that are 1 by 1, 3 by 3, 5 by 5, 7 by 7, and 9 by 9.

Tips for the Linguistically Diverse Classroom

Diagram Code The Diagram Code technique is described in detail in *Getting to Know Connected Mathematics*. Students use a minimal number of words and drawings, diagrams, or symbols to respond to questions that require writing. Example: Question 1—A student might answer this question by drawing a three-layered ziggurat with the layers labeled *A, B, C* from bottom to top. The student might draw an arrow, labeled *square*, pointing to the perimeter outline, and write *B* < *A, C* < *B* beneath the drawing.

TEACHING THE INVESTIGATION

5.1 • Building Ziggurats

This investigation makes an interesting connection between geometry and number theory—square numbers, even and odd numbers, and their relation to ziggurats.

Launch

Show the following base plan on the board or overhead, and ask students to build a model of the plan with their partners.

1	1	1	1	1
1	2	2	2	1
1	2	3	2	1
1	2	2	2	1
1	1	1	1	1

When students are finished, remove the base plan from view.

> Look at the tower you have built. How can you describe it in words?
> (*It is like a tiered cake, except each layer is a square.*)

> This kind of tower is called a *ziggurat*. Ziggurats were built in ancient times by the Assyrians and Babylonians.

Now display this base plan, and ask groups to build the model it represents.

2	2	2
2	5	2
2	2	2

> This tower is also a ziggurat. What do you think the rules, or constraints, are for what makes a building a ziggurat? (*A ziggurat is a tiered building with square layers. Each square layer is smaller than the layer below it.*)

Go over the problem and follow-up with students to make sure they know what is expected of them.

Explore

As students work, look for those who have clever ways of thinking about follow-up question 2, and make sure these ideas are shared during the summary. Ask students who are ready for an extra challenge how many cubes are needed to build the tenth or the nth layer of a ziggurat.

Summarize

Call on some students to present their building plans and to explain what their groups found in the follow-up. Encourage other students to ask questions of the presenters.

As a class, resolve any differences about the number of cubes needed for each layer of a three-, four-, or five-layer ziggurat. Help students recognize the patterns in these numbers.

> Starting from the top of a five-layer ziggurat, how many cubes are in each layer? (*1, 9, 25, 49, and 81*)
>
> What kinds of numbers are these? (*square numbers*)
>
> What number times itself equals 1? (*1*) What number times itself equals 9? (*3*) What number times itself equals 25? (*5*) 49? (*7*) 81? (*9*) What kinds of numbers are these? (*They are all odd numbers.*) If a ziggurat had six layers, how many cubes would be in the sixth layer? (*121*)
>
> The dimensions of the layers are 1 by 1, 3 by 3, 5 by 5, and so on. Why does each dimension increase by 2 with each layer? Could you build a ziggurat so that each dimension only increases by 1 with each layer? Why or why not?

Students should see that if you require that the outer edge of each layer not be covered by the cubes above it, the dimensions must increase by 2 for each layer.

5.2 • Representing Ziggurats

It may be appropriate at this time to remind the class that Emily found that Montarekians always built maximal buildings.

Launch

Tell the class about Emily's discovery.

> Emily Hawkins discovered that some ziggurats in ancient Montarek had layers that were more than one story high.

Refer students to Problem 5.2 in their books, or display Transparency 5.2.

> In this problem, you will build two ziggurats from base plans that Emily found. For the first ziggurat, you will draw a set of building plans. For the second, you will make a drawing on isometric dot paper. When you finish your drawings, write a short paragraph about which representation you think is most useful for describing a ziggurat.

Have students work in groups of five to construct the buildings, but ask that they work on the representations of the buildings on their own.

> When you are finished, share your answers with your group. You can revise your answers if you have new ideas after the group discussion.

Explore

As you circulate, ask questions that encourage students to contemplate what information about a building is gained or lost with each type of representation.

> What are the advantages of using a cube model? What are the disadvantages?
>
> What are the advantages of using a set of building plans? What are the disadvantages?
>
> What are the advantages of using an isometric drawing? What are the disadvantages?
>
> If you wanted to give someone directions for building a ziggurat, which representation would be best?

Summarize

Have several students share their opinions and arguments about which representation is most useful. Be sure the pros and cons of each representation are discussed.

> What is useful about a cube model? (*There are no hidden cubes. You can turn it and see all sides.*) What makes the cube model awkward? (*It takes time to build it each time you want to show it to someone, and it is hard to transport.*)
>
> What is useful about an isometric drawing? (*It shows you what the building looks like from a corner so you can get a sense of the building's structure.*) What are the disadvantages of the isometric drawing? (*You can't turn it to see what the other corners look like, and you must count carefully to get an idea of how to build it.*)
>
> What is useful about a set of building plans? (*It shows you exactly what the base layer looks like, and you can easily see how the layers are constructed.*) What are the disadvantages of a set of building plans? (*Cubes can be hidden from the views shown in the plans.*)

Additional Answers

Answers to Problem 5.1

B.

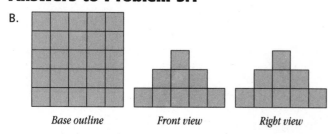

Base outline   Front view   Right view

Answers to Problem 5.2

A.

Base outline

Front view

Right view

B.

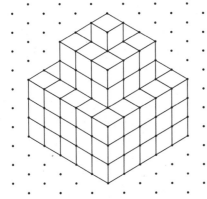

Answer to Problem 5.2 Follow-Up

Possible answer:

2	2	2	2	2
2	5	5	5	2
2	5	7	5	2
2	5	5	5	2
2	2	2	2	2

Front

Seeing the Isometric View

This investigation focuses on sharpening students' visualization skills. In Problem 6.1, Viewing a Building, students match cube buildings to isometric views from various corners of the structures. In Problem 6.2, Removing Cubes, they visualize what buildings would look like if certain cubes were removed. In Problem 6.3, Adding Cubes, they visualize what buildings would look like if cubes were added. In Problem 6.4, Putting the Pieces Together, they solve visual puzzles, manipulating two puzzle pieces to form given figures.

Mathematical and Problem-Solving Goals

- **To develop an efficient strategy for reading information from isometric drawings in order to match buildings with their corner views**

- **To reason visually and analytically about cube buildings**

- **To visualize how a cube building will change when cubes are added or removed**

- **To solve visual puzzles by determining how two basic shapes can combine to form a given shape**

- **To create puzzles for others to solve**

	Materials	
Problem	**For students**	**For the teacher**
All	Calculators, cubes (20 per student), building mats, isometric dot paper, sugar cubes (optional; for homework)	Transparencies 6.1 to 6.4 (optional), cubes, transparent isometric dot paper (provided as a blackline master)
6.1	Labsheet 6.1 (1 per student)	Transparency of Labsheet 6.1
6.2	2-D design cubes (from Labsheet 4.2)	
6.4	Labsheet 6.4 (1 per student)	

Student Pages 72–81   Teaching the Investigation 81a–81h

Grouping:
Small Groups

Launch

- Form groups of three, and ask each student in each group to construct one of the three buildings in the problem.

- Discuss how to name corner views by using the building mat labels.

Explore

- Circulate as students individually match corner views with the buildings and then compare answers within their groups.

- Ask questions about how cubes can be hidden in a corner view.

Summarize

- In a class discussion, let students share strategies for matching views to buildings.

- Review the idea of hidden cubes.

Assignment Choices

ACE question 1 and unassigned choices from earlier problems

INVESTIGATION 6

Seeing the Isometric View

This investigation will help you improve your ability to read isometric drawings. During this investigation, you will have the opportunity to think about the following:

- How can a drawing help you to visualize the building it describes?
- Can you use your imagination to visualize what a building will look like after some small alteration is made to it?

6.1 Viewing a Building

You have learned to draw isometric representations showing each of the four corners of a building. But can you interpret a drawing that someone else has done? Can you compare the drawing to cube models and identify which model it describes? Can you determine which corner of the building is shown in the picture?

Problem 6.1

In your group, build a cube model of each of these buildings on your building mat. The next page shows views of each building from all four corners. These views also appear on Labsheet 6.1. Match each model to its corner views. On the labsheet, label each view with the building number and the corner from which the building is being viewed: left front, front right, back left, or right back.

Building 1

1	1	2
	3	1
	1	

Front

Building 2

1	1	2
1	3	
	1	

Front

Building 3

1	2	1
	3	1
	2	

Front

Answers to Problem 6.1

A. Building 1, front right

B. Building 2, left front

C. Building 1, right back

D. Building 3, right back

E. Building 1, back left

F. Building 2, back left

G. Building 2, right back

H. Building 3, front right

I. Building 3, left front

J. Building 1, left front

K. Building 3, back left

L. Building 2, front right

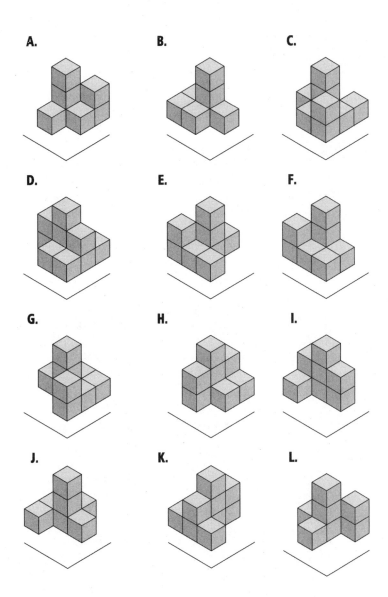

A.

B.

C.

D.

E.

F.

G.

H.

I.

J.

K.

L.

■ **Problem 6.1 Follow-Up**

Can you remove a cube from building 1 and have the isometric view from any corner still be the same? What about building 2 and building 3?

Investigation 6: Seeing the Isometric View **73**

Answer to Problem 6.1 Follow-Up

Building 1: Since a stack of three cubes can hide a stack of two cubes, you could remove a cube from the two-cube stack in the back right corner without affecting the view from the left front (view J). Since a stack of three cubes can hide a single cube, you could remove the cube in the back left corner without affecting the view from the front right corner (view A).

Building 2: You could remove a cube from the two-cube stack in the back right corner without affecting view B or remove the cube from the back left corner without affecting view L.

Building 3: In addition to the options listed for building 1 (affecting views I and H), you could remove the cube to the right of the three-cube stack. In the left front view (view I), this cube is hidden by the two-cube stack in the front row.

Removing Cubes

At a Glance

Grouping:
As a Class

Launch

- Do part A of the problem as a class, having students visualize what the new building would look like and then check their answers by constructing the building and removing the indicated cubes.

Explore

- Have students make drawings individually and then check their answers with their partners.

- Assist students who are having trouble seeing the isometric views.

Summarize

- In a class discussion, ask students to share their strategies for visualizing the changes in the buildings.

6.2 Removing Cubes

In this problem, you will play with a building in your mind to visualize what it would look like if you removed cubes from it. As you work on this problem, remember that you can always build a cube model to check your imagination—but give your mind a try first. You will be surprised at how much you can improve your visualization skills by thinking hard about the problems and by practicing visualizing things in your mind.

Problem 6.2

In each drawing given, visualize what the figure would look like if the orange cubes were removed. Make an isometric drawing of the result. If you need to, build the model from cubes and look at it.

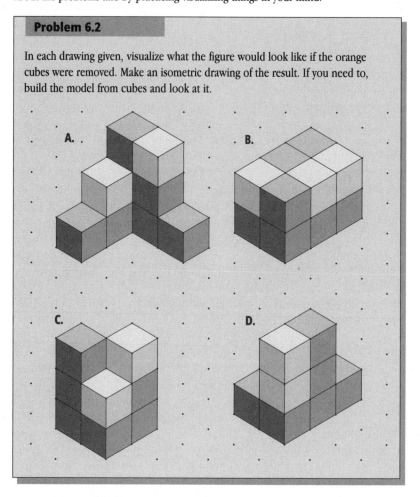

■ **Problem 6.2 Follow-Up**

Look carefully at A–D. Can you find a different possibility for what the building would look like with orange cubes removed?

Assignment Choices

ACE questions 2, 5, 7, and unassigned choices from earlier problems

Answers to Problem 6.2

See page 81f.

Answer to Problem 6.2 Follow-Up

Every one of the buildings could have at least one hidden cube that would show when the orange cubes were removed.

6.3 Adding Cubes

In the last problem, you imagined what cube buildings would look like if some cubes were removed. In this problem, you will imagine what buildings will look like if cubes are added. Remember to try to do the problem without cubes first. Then, you can build a model to check your work.

Problem 6.3

In each drawing, one or more cube faces are orange. Picture what the model would look like with a cube added to each orange face. Make an isometric drawing of the result.

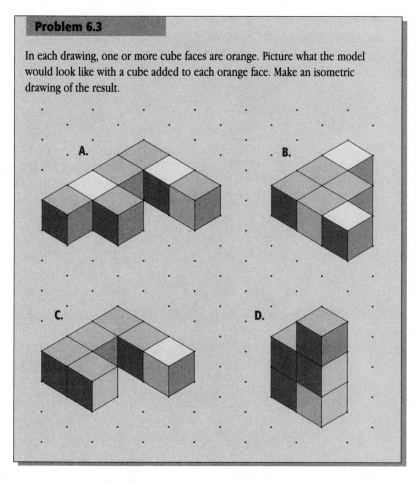

▨ Problem 6.3 Follow-Up

Which is harder for you to visualize and draw without building a cube model, adding or removing a cube? Explain why you think this is so.

At a Glance

Grouping:
Individuals or Pairs

Launch

■ Do part A of the problem as a class, having students construct the building, add the indicated cubes, and make an isometric drawing of the new building.

Explore

■ Have students make drawings individually and then check their answers with their partners.

■ Assist students who are having trouble seeing the isometric views.

Summarize

■ In a class discussion, ask students to share their strategies for visualizing the changes in the buildings.

Answers to Problem 6.3

See page 81f.

Answer to Problem 6.3 Follow-Up

Answers will vary. For many students, visualizing the addition of cubes is more difficult than visualizing their removal.

Assignment Choices

ACE question 3 and unassigned choices from earlier problems

Putting the Pieces Together

Grouping: Individuals

Launch

- Create the two basic shapes from cubes, and demonstrate to the class how they can be combined.

- Hand out Labsheet 6.4.

Explore

- Have students work on the problems individually and then check answers with their partners.

- As students finish, have them move to the follow-up.

- Assign ACE question 4 to students ready for an additional challenge.

Summarize

- Ask students to share their experiences with deciphering the puzzles.

- Have students exchange the puzzles they created in the follow-up.

Assignment Choices

ACE questions 4, 6, and unassigned choices from earlier problems

Assessment

It is appropriate to use Check-Up 2 and the Quiz after this problem.

6.4 Putting the Pieces Together

In this problem, you will look at several buildings made from these two basic shapes:

Your challenge is to figure out how these two shapes were put together to make each building.

   ⟶

Problem 6.4

In A–F, experiment with the two basic shapes above to make the building shown. Shade the drawings on your labsheet to show how you put the pieces together to make the shape.

A.   **B.**   **C.**

D.   **E.**   **F.**

■ Problem 6.4 Follow-Up

Put the two basic shapes together in a way not shown above. Make an isometric drawing of your model.

Answers to Problem 6.4

See page 81f.

Answer to Problem 6.4 Follow-Up

Answers will vary.

Applications

1. On a building mat, use cubes to make a model of this building.

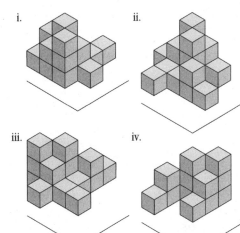

a. For each picture below, indicate from which corner you are viewing the building.

i. ii.

iii. iv.

Answers

Applications

1a.

i. front right

ii. back left

iii. right back

iv. left front

1b. See page 81g.

1c. no

2. There are four possible answers; here's one:

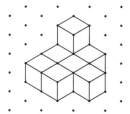

3.

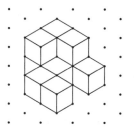

4. Answers will vary.

b. Remove a cube from each of the three stacks in the front row of the base plan. Make isometric drawings of all four corners of this new building.

c. Do any of the corner views stay the same as the corresponding corner view on the original building?

2. Visualize what this model would look like with the orange cubes removed. Draw an isometric view of the resulting model from the same corner as the original drawing was made.

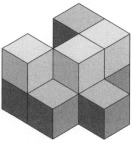

3. Visualize what this model would look like if cubes were added to the orange faces. Draw an isometric view of the resulting model from the same corner as the original model was made.

4. Design your own two basic shapes. Use four or five cubes for each shape. Put the shapes together to make a new model. Draw the shapes and the new model on isometric dot paper so that you can challenge a classmate to find how you put the two pieces together.

Connections

5. Talk to your art teacher, a drafting teacher, or an architect about the kind of drawings they make. Report on the similarities and differences between their drawings and the kinds of drawings you have made in this unit.

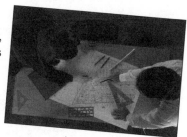

Extensions

6. Here is a drawing of a simple model made from cubes:

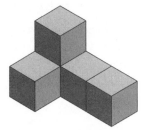

    a. How many cubes are in the model?

    b. What is the perimeter of the base of the model?

Imagine a model just like the one above but with each of its edge lengths doubled.

    c. How many cubes would it take to build the new model?

    d. What is the perimeter of the base of the new model?

    e. Make an isometric drawing of the new model from the same corner the drawing of the original model was made from.

6e.

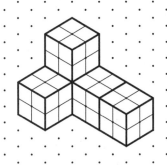

Connections
5. Answers will vary.

Extensions
6a. 5 cubes

6b. 10 units

6c. 40 cubes; Each cube becomes a 2 by 2 by 2 cube, so the new building has 8 times the number of cubes that the original building had.

6d. 20 units

6e. See below left.

7a. This building could have from 17 to 34 cubes. Some students may argue that the minimum is 16 cubes, but this gives a base that is only connected on a corner.

7b.

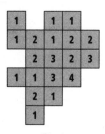

Front

7c.

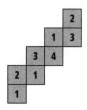

Front

7. a. The building below is shown from the front right corner. How many cubes would it take to make this building? If there is more than one answer, give the least and the greatest numbers of cubes that could be used.

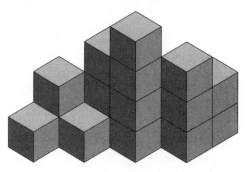

b. Make a base plan for a building made with the minimum number of cubes.

c. Make a base plan for the building made with the maximum number of cubes.

Mathematical Reflections

In this investigation, you have worked on visualizing corner views of buildings, even when the buildings are changed by adding or removing cubes. These questions will help you summarize what you have learned:

1. Summarize how you look at a model built from cubes to see the model in a way that can be drawn on isometric dot paper.

2. If you make an isometric drawing of a model from each of its four corners, will your drawings determine a unique building? Explain why or why not. You may want to use an example in your explanation.

Think about your answers to these questions, discuss your ideas with other students and your teacher, and then write a summary of your findings in your journal.

Possible Answers

1. I look at a cube that has a vertex on the corner I am facing, and I move my eye until I see a hexagon with that vertex in the exact center. I adjust until I see each visible cube as three rhombuses that are the same size. I also think about what cubes will be hidden by taller stacks in front.

2. No, it will not always make a unique building. There is still the possibility that cubes are hidden in the center of the building so that I cannot see them from any of the corners. To make an example of this, you need to make tall outside stacks and a short, hidden inside area.

Tips for the Linguistically Diverse Classroom

Original Rebus The Original Rebus technique is described in detail in *Getting to Know Connected Mathematics*. Students make a copy of the text before it is discussed. During discussion, they generate their own rebuses for words they do not understand as the words are made comprehensible through pictures, objects, or demonstrations. Example: Question 2— key words for which students may make rebuses are *isometric* (isometric pattern of dots), *four corners* (a base plan with an arrow pointing to each corner), *unique* (the number 1), *building* (a cube building).

TEACHING THE INVESTIGATION

6.1 • Viewing a Building

This investigation helps build students' ability to visualize a building from a drawing, and then visualize changes made to that building.

Launch

Arrange students into groups of three. Refer them to Problem 6.1 in their books, or display Transparency 6.1.

> I would like each group to put together the three buildings shown in the problem. Make each building on a separate building mat.

As groups assemble the buildings, pass out a copy of Labsheet 6.1 to each student.

> Now you will match the corner views of your buildings with the drawings on Labsheet 6.1.

> Use the labels on your building mat to help you identify the corner at which you are looking. Label the drawings on the worksheet with both the building number and the corner. Two labels on your building mat correspond to each corner, so your corner labels will consist of two words: front right, right back, back left, or left front.

Demonstrate how to use the labels on the mat. To name a corner, list the building mat labels from left to right.

> Work by yourself on this activity. Each person in your group can start with a different building. Then, switch mats until everyone has worked with all three buildings.

> When everyone in your group has finished, compare your answers and resolve any differences you have.

Explore

Circulate as students work. Encourage them to position a corner cube of the building they are inspecting so that they see one vertex in the exact center of six surrounding vertices. Remind students that, on isometric dot paper, the outer edges of a cube form a hexagon, with the center vertex of the cube in the center of the hexagon—and this is exactly what they should see when positioning a building. You might suggest that students who are having trouble view the buildings with one eye closed.

Ask questions about hidden cubes.

> What is the tallest stack of cubes that can be hidden by a stack of three cubes?

A stack of two cubes can be hidden by a stack of three cubes if, from the view in question, the two-cube stack is positioned to touch the back corner of the three-cube stack. You may need to help some students understand this by studying their buildings with them. For example, consider the base plan for building 1.

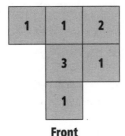

Front

When viewed from the left front corner, the two-cube stack is hidden by the three-cube stack.

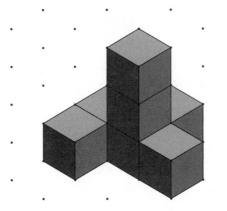

Summarize

Review the answers, and help students resolve any problems. You can record the answers on a transparency of Labsheet 6.1. Allow students to describe the strategies they used to match the views to the buildings.

Discuss the fact that cubes can be hidden in the isometric drawings. A good model to use for demonstrating is this base plan, in which 15 cubes are hidden in the front right view:

1	1	1		
1	2	2	2	
1	2	3	3	3
	2	3	3	3
		3	3	3

Front

6.2 • Removing Cubes

Imagination and visualization are important aspects of these problems. Students should try to visualize first, and then make the building as a check of their work.

Launch

A good way to launch this problem is to go through part A with the class.

> Imagine that the orange cubes in the building in part A were removed. Make a drawing on isometric dot paper of what the new building would look like.

> Try using your imagination first, but if you have trouble, use your cubes to make the building and then remove the indicated cubes.

After students have made their drawings, have each student or pair construct the building to check their work.

> Now, I would like you to work in your pairs on the rest of the problems. Try to do each part in your head, then check your answers by using your cubes.

Explore

Students should make their own drawings and then work with their partners to verify their answers and resolve any differences.

Use this time to help students who are still having trouble seeing as the dot paper sees. Remind them that they can use their 2-D design cubes to build the figure on isometric dot paper and then remove the appropriate 2-D cubes to see the results.

Summarize

In a class discussion, ask students to share their answers and the strategies they used to visualize how the buildings would change. Some may have visualized the changes in their minds. Some may have built cube models and removed the indicated cubes. Others may have used the 2-D design cubes and worked directly on the isometric dot paper.

6.3 • Adding Cubes

Visualization exercises continue as students now add cubes to buildings.

Launch

Refer students to Problem 6.3 in their books, or display Transparency 6.3.

> In the last problem, you looked at isometric drawings of cube buildings and imagined what the buildings would look like if certain cubes were removed from them. In this problem, you will visualize how buildings would look if cubes were *added* to certain faces.

Assemble the building in part A on your building mat. Now, add a cube to each of the orange faces, and look carefully at the result.

Your challenge is to make an isometric drawing of the new building from the same corner as that shown in the problem.

After students have made and checked their drawings, let them continue on their own.

I would like you to work in your pairs on parts B, C, and D. Before you construct the buildings, try to visualize what they would look like if cubes were added to the faces that are orange in the drawing. You can then make the buildings to check your mind's picture.

Explore

Use this time to help students who are still having trouble. Remind them that they can use their 2-D design cubes to build the figure on isometric dot paper and then add the appropriate 2-D cubes.

Summarize

In a class discussion, go over the answers. Allow students to share the strategies they used to visualize how the buildings would change.

6.4 • Putting the Pieces Together

This problem presents several puzzles in which students must determine how two basic cube shapes can be joined to form a given building. You may want to refer to the building activities of Problem 4.3 in order to help.

Launch

Before class, make a model of each basic shape by taping cubes together or using interlocking cubes. If possible, use a different color for each shape.

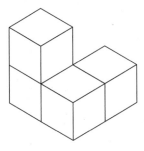

Hold up the two shapes.

These two basic shapes can fit together in lots of ways.

Demonstrate by combining the pieces in several different ways to form new figures.

Pass out a copy of Labsheet 6.4 to each student.

> Each of the buildings in these isometric drawings was created from these two basic shapes. Your challenge is to figure out how the basic shapes were put together to form each building.
>
> Shade the figures on the labsheet to show how the shapes fit together. You only need to shade one of the basic shapes; the unshaded cubes should form the other basic shape.

Have students work on the problem individually, comparing answers with their partners.

Explore

Some students will need to tape cubes together to make the basic shapes (using a different color for each basic shape), then physically put them together to make the buildings. When students finish, have them work on the follow-up.

Assign ACE question 4 to students who are ready for an extra challenge. This question asks them to design their own basic shapes and combine them to form a new building. They draw their basic shapes and their building on isometric dot paper, then challenge a classmate to figure out how the shapes were put together.

Summarize

Ask students what was hard and what was easy in figuring out the puzzles. You might use the ideas in the Mathematical Reflections on page 81 as a part of this summary.

If students did the follow-up, have them exchange their isometric drawings with a partner.

Additional Answers

Answers to Problem 6.2

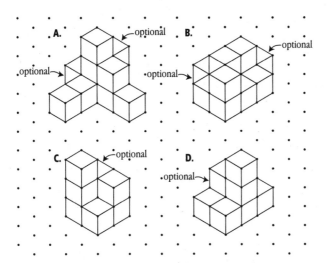

Answers to Problem 6.3

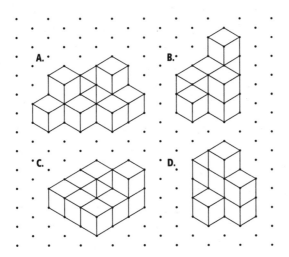

Answers to Problem 6.4

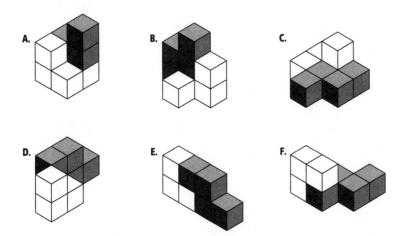

ACE Answers

Applications

1b.

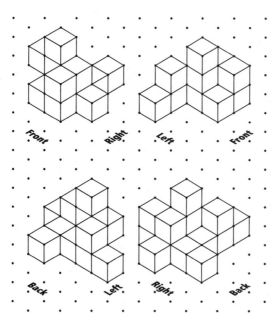

Assigning the Unit Project

The unit project, Design a Building, is an integral part of the assessment in *Ruins of Montarek*. The project asks students to put to use all the skills they have developed for representing three-dimensional objects with two-dimensional drawings.

Students are to imagine that they are architects in ancient Montarek. Each student must design a building that he or she feels would be useful to the citizens of Montarek. Each student should prepare a cube model, a base plan, a set of building plans, and four isometric drawings of the building. A project should also include a letter to the Council of Montarek explaining how the building will be used and how it will benefit the citizens of Montarek.

If you do not have enough cubes for all students, we recommend that they work with sugar cubes. The sugar-cube models can be glued together and displayed. If your students use wooden cubes, you may have to work out a schedule for them to construct their models so that the whole class isn't using cubes at the same time.

A sample of a student project and a suggested scoring rubric are given in the Assessment Resources section.

Design a Building

According to the diary of an architect in ancient Montarek, a building had to be approved by the Council of Montarek before it could be constructed. To have a building approved, an architect had to provide the council with a base plan, a set of building plans, and isometric sketches of the building.

Imagine that you are an architect in ancient Montarek. Design a building that you feel would be useful to the citizens of Montarek. The building does not have to be a ziggurat or any of the other buildings you have studied. This is your opportunity to design a building that *you* think is interesting.

You must follow these steps to have your building approved by the Council of Montarek:

1. Use 25 to 30 cubes to design your building.
2. Make a base plan of your building on grid paper.
3. Make a set of building plans for your building on grid paper.
4. Make four sketches of your building on isometric dot paper—one sketch from each corner.
5. Write a paragraph to the Council of Montarek explaining how your building could be used and why it would benefit the citizens of Montarek.

Assessment Resources

Check-Up 1

1. The right view of a building is given below. Which of the views is the left view? _____

a.
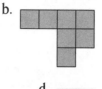

b.
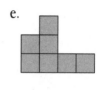

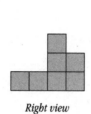

Right view

c.
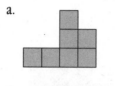

d.

e.

In 2 and 3, use the base plan and views shown below.

a.

b.

e.
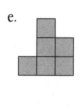

2		
3	1	2
1		1

Front

c.
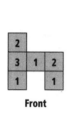

d.

2. Picture the building that the base plan describes. Which view is the front view of the building? _____

3. Picture the building that the base plan describes. Which view is the right view of the building? _____

Check-Up 1

4. A base plan for a building is given at right.
On the grids below, draw a set of building plans—
a base outline, a front view, and a right view—
for the building.

Front

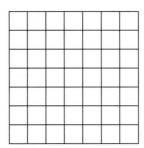  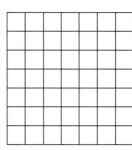

Base outline	*Front view*	*Right view*

5. The base outline, front view, and right view of a building are given below. On the grid, draw a base plan for a building that fits this set of plans.

   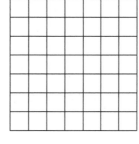

Base outline	*Front view*	*Right view*

6. Picture a building that has the front and right views shown below.
  • Draw the base outline of your building.
  • Create a base plan by numbering the squares of your base outline.

 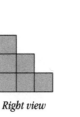 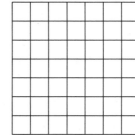

Front view	*Right view*

Name _____ Date _____

7. Look at the set of building plans shown below.

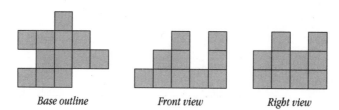

Base outline   Front view   Right view

a. On the grid below, draw a base plan for a *minimal building* that fits the building plans. How many cubes are needed to construct a minimal building for these plans? _____

b. Now draw a base plan for a *maximal building* that fits the building plans. How many cubes are needed to construct a maximal building for these plans? _____

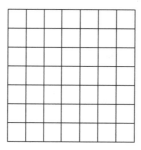

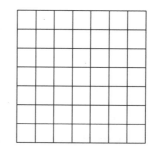

Minimal building   Maximal building

Check-Up 2

1. Which isometric drawing shows the view from the left front corner of the building represented by the base plan below? _____

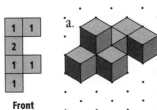

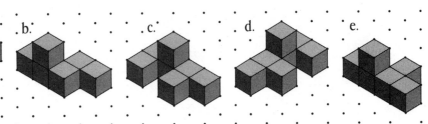

2. Which isometric drawing shows the view from the back left corner of the building represented by the base plan below? _____

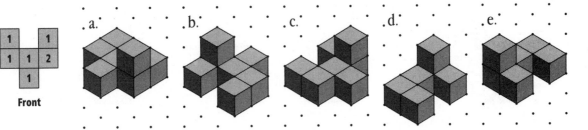

3. Which drawing is not a view of the building shown below? _____

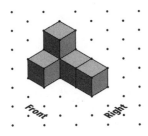

a.   b.   c.   d.   e.

Check-Up 2

4. The isometric drawing below shows a building from the front right corner. Which drawing shows the back view of the building? _____

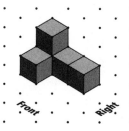

a.   b.   c.   d.   e.

5. The isometric drawing below shows a building from the front right corner. Which drawing shows the right view of the building? _____

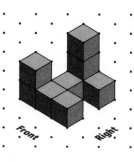

a.   b.   c.   d.   e.

6. Draw the isometric view from the right back corner of the building represented by the base plan below.

1		
2	1	
3	2	1

Front

Check-Up 2

7. Draw the building that would remain if the shaded cubes were removed from the building below.

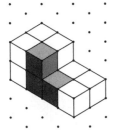

8. Which of the buildings below can be made from the two basic shapes shown?

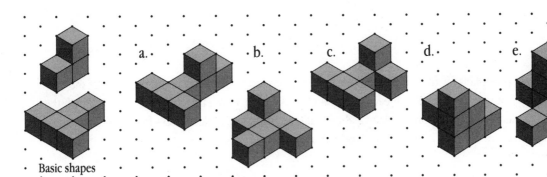

Basic shapes   a.   b.   c.   d.   e.

9. How many cubes are needed to build this rectangular solid?

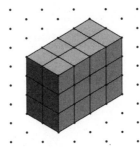

Quiz

1. In her last expedition to Montarek, Emily Hawkins found a stone tablet containing this set of building plans.

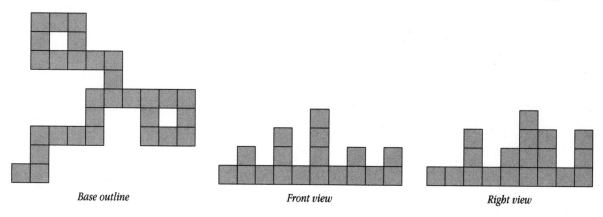

Base outline   *Front view*   *Right view*

   a. Construct a maximal building for this set of plans. Make a base plan of your building by numbering the squares in the base outline.

   b. How many cubes did your building require? _____

2. Below are base plans for three different buildings. The next page shows isometric drawings of the three buildings from each corner. Match each building with its corner views. Label each corner view with the building number and the corner—front right, right back, back left, or left front—from which the building is being viewed. Put your labels on the lines provided.

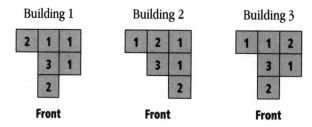

Building 1   Building 2   Building 3

Quiz

a. Building _____

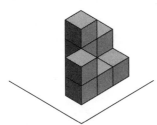

b. Building _____

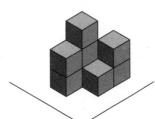

c. Building _____

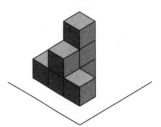

d. Building _____

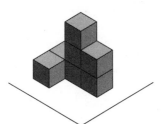

e. Building _____

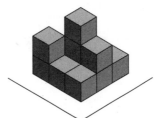

f. Building _____

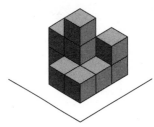

g. Building _____

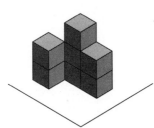

h. Building _____

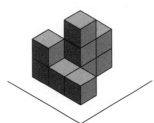

i. Building _____

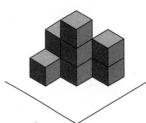

j. Building _____

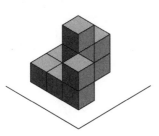

k. Building _____

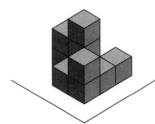

l. Building _____

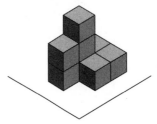

Assign these questions as additional homework, or use them as review, quiz, or test questions.

In 1 and 2, draw the mirror image of the figure on the other side of the mirror line.

1.

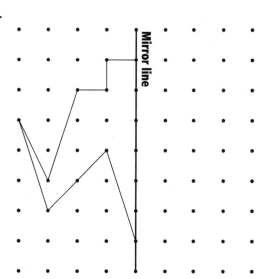

2.

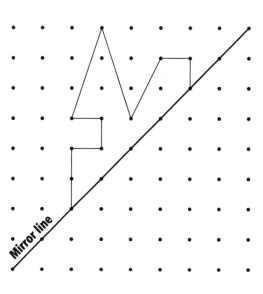

3. The base plan of a building is given below. Which of the given views is the left view? _____

Front

a.

b.

c.

d.

e.

4. The back view of a building is given below. Which of the given views is the front view? _____

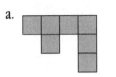

a.

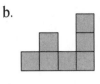

b.

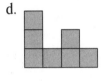

e.

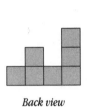

Back view

c.

d.

5. Below is a set of building plans.

Base outline

Front view

Right view

Which of the base plans below can be completed to match the building in the plans? _____

a.

b.

c.

d.

e.

6. The base outline and front view of a building are given at right. Which of the views below could be a left view of the building? _____

Base outline   *Front view*

a.

b.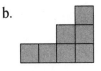

e.

c.

d.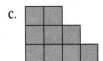

7. How many different views of the shape below can be drawn on isometric dot paper if the shape can be turned freely? _____

Draw as many views of the shape as you can on isometric dot paper.

8. Which of the buildings below can be made from the two basic shapes shown? _____

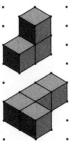

a.

b.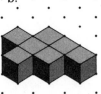

c.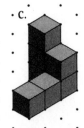

d.

e.

Basic shapes

9. **a.** What is the maximum number of cubes that could be used to make the building below? _____

  b. What is the minimum number of cubes needed to make the building below? _____

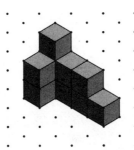

10. One view of a building is given at left below. From the drawings, find another view of the building. _____

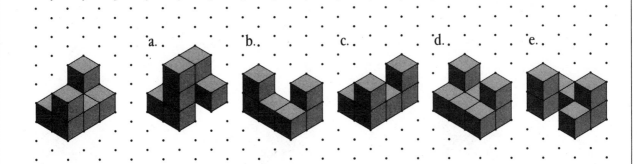

                  a.   b.   c.   d.   e.

11. A base plan of a building is given below. Which of the following is *not* a corner view of the building? _____

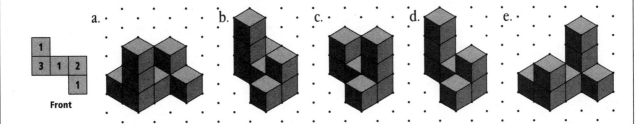

   a.   b.   c.   d.   e.

Front

12. If a cube were added to the white face of the building given below, what would the new building look like?

_____

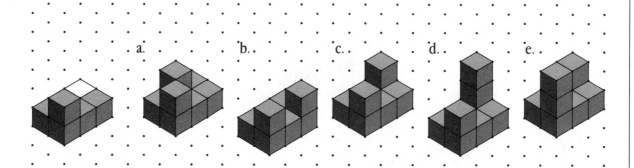

13. If the white cubes were removed from the building shown below, what would the new building look like?

_____

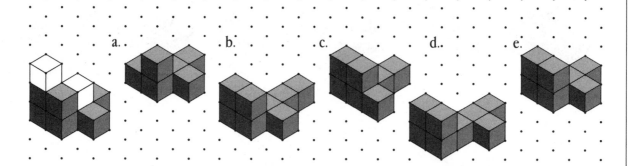

Unit Test

1. Using your cubes, make a model of the building shown in this base plan:

Front

   a. Sketch a set of building plans for the building on grid paper. Remember that a set of building plans includes the base outline, the front view, and the right view.

   b. Add as many cubes as you can to the building to make a different building that has the same set of building plans. Make a base plan of your new building.

   c. Explain how your new building can have the same set of building plans as the original building even though your new building has a different base plan.

2. The base outline and right view of a building are shown below. Of the three different front views below, which view is not a possible front view for a building that has the base outline and right view? Explain your reasoning.

Base outline

Right view

a.

Front view

b.

Front view

c.

Front view

3. Melinda has sketched this set of building plans on grid paper:

Base outline

Front view

Right view

   a. Melinda claims that she can make a building with 12 cubes that fits the above set of plans. Sketch a base plan of a building that uses 12 cubes that fits Melinda's set of building plans.

   b. Do you think that your base plan is exactly the same as the base plan for Melinda's building? Explain why or why not.

   c. Could you use more than 12 cubes to make a building that fits Melinda's building plans? If so, what is the greatest number of cubes you could use for a building that fits Melinda's building plans? If not, explain why 12 cubes is the greatest number of cubes you can use to make a building that fits Melinda's building plans.

Unit Test

4. For each of the cube buildings shown below, make a sketch on isometric dot paper of what the building would look like if the shaded cube(s) were removed.

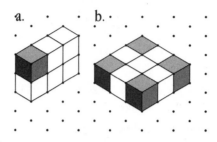

a.　　　b.

5. Make a sketch on isometric dot paper to show what the building made from the base plan below would look like.

3	3	3
3	3	3
3	3	3

Name _____ Date _____

Journal Organization

_____ Problems and Mathematical Reflections are labeled and dated.

_____ Work is neat and easy to find and follow.

Vocabulary

_____ All words are listed.

_____ All words are defined or described.

Quizzes and Check-Ups

_____ Check-Up 1   _____ Quiz   _____ Check-Up 2   _____ Unit Test

Homework Assignments

_____ _____

_____ _____

_____ _____

_____ _____

_____ _____

_____ _____

_____ _____

_____ _____

_____ _____

_____ _____

_____ _____

_____ _____

_____ _____

Self-Assessment

Vocabulary

Of the vocabulary words I defined or described in my journal, the word _____ best demonstrates my ability to give a clear definition or description.

Of the vocabulary words I defined or described in my journal, the word _____ best demonstrates my ability to use an example to help explain or describe an idea.

Mathematical Ideas

1. **a.** In *Ruins of Montarek*, I developed these skills for representing three-dimensional objects on paper:

   b. Here are page numbers of journal entries that give evidence of what I have learned, along with descriptions of what each entry shows:

2. **a.** These are the spatial skills I am still struggling with:

   b. This is why I think these ideas are difficult for me:

   c. Here are page numbers of journal entries that give evidence of what I am struggling with, along with descriptions of what each entry shows:

Class Participation

I contributed to the classroom discussion and understanding of *Ruins of Montarek* when I...
(Give examples.)

Answer Keys

Answers to Check-Up 1

1. e

2. c

3. e

4.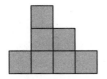

   Base outline   *Front view*   *Right view*

5.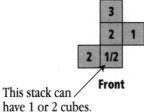

   This stack can have 1 or 2 cubes.

6. These diagrams show the minimal base outline and the maximal base outline. Many other base outlines are possible.

   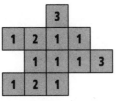   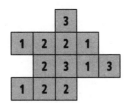

   Front   **Front**
   Minimal building   Maximal building

7. a. 18

   b. 23

Answers to Check-Up 2

1. e

2. b

3. c

4. d

5. b

6.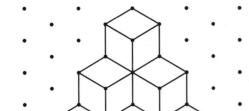

7.

8. d

9. 24

Answers to Quiz

1. a.

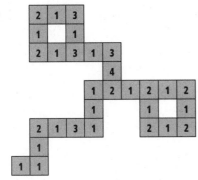

Front

   b. 49

2. a. building 2, front right   **b.** building 3, front right   **c.** building 2, back left

   d. building 3, left front   **e.** building 2, right back   **f.** building 1, right back

   g. building 1, left front   **h.** building 3, back left   **i.** building 2, left front

   j. building 1, back left   **k.** building 3, right back   **l.** building 1, front right

Answers to Question Bank

1.

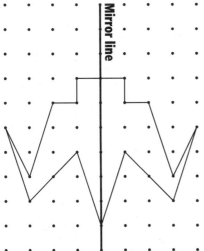

2.

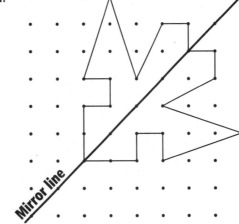

3. a

4. d

5. a

6. a

7. 12

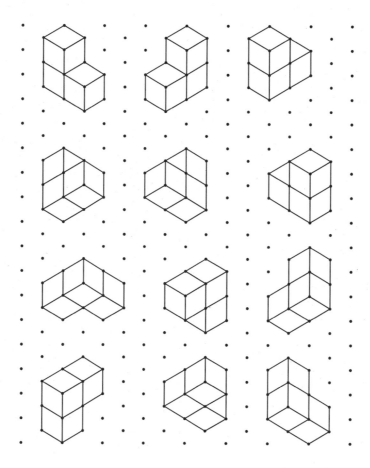

8. c

9. **a.** 15

    b. 10

10. e

11. d

12. c

13. e

Answer Keys

Answers to the Unit Test

1. a.

   Base outline   *Front view*   *Right view*

   b. Possible answer:

   Front

   c. The original building is not a maximal building and, therefore, is not necessarily unique. The base plan shown in part b above is a maximal building for the plans in part a.

2. Front view c is not a possible front view of the building.

3. a. Possible answer:

   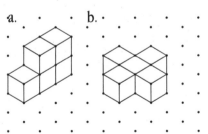

   Front

   b. Probably not since the building in part a is not unique and so there are other possibilities for Melinda's building (for example, the 1 and 2 can be interchanged in any row of the base plan and the building will still fit Melinda's set of building plans).

   c. The greatest number of cubes that could be used is 16—by placing 2 cubes in each position of the base plan. This would be the unique maximal building for Melinda's set of building plans.

4. a.   b.

   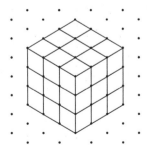

5. Students should sketch a $3 \times 3 \times 3$ cube made from 27 unit cubes:

The unit project for *Ruins of Montarek* is the Design a Building Project. A possible scoring rubric and a sample project with teacher comments are given here.

Suggested Scoring Rubric

Drawing
Base plan—3 points
- outline of base is correct (1 pt)
- numbers match heights of cube stacks (2 pts)

Set of building plans—6 points
- base outline is accurate (2 pts)
- front view is accurate (2 pts)
- right view is accurate (2 pts)

Isometric views—12 points
- front right corner is accurate (3 pts)
- right back corner is accurate (3 pts)
- back left corner is accurate (3 pts)
- left front corner is accurate (3 pts)

Letter
Composition—3 points
- letter is clear, easy to read, and makes sense (1 pt)
- explanation is given for the building's use (1 pt)
- justification is given for why the design should be chosen (1 pt)

Structure—2 points
- work is neat (1 pt)
- grammar and spelling are correct (1 pt)

Project Constraints
- 25–30 cubes are used (1 pt)
- model is used to represent the building (1 pt)
- work is neat and organized (1 pt)
- presentation is appropriate (1 pt)

Sample Project

Front Right

Right Back

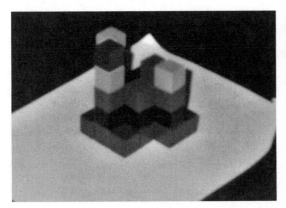

Back Left

Left Front

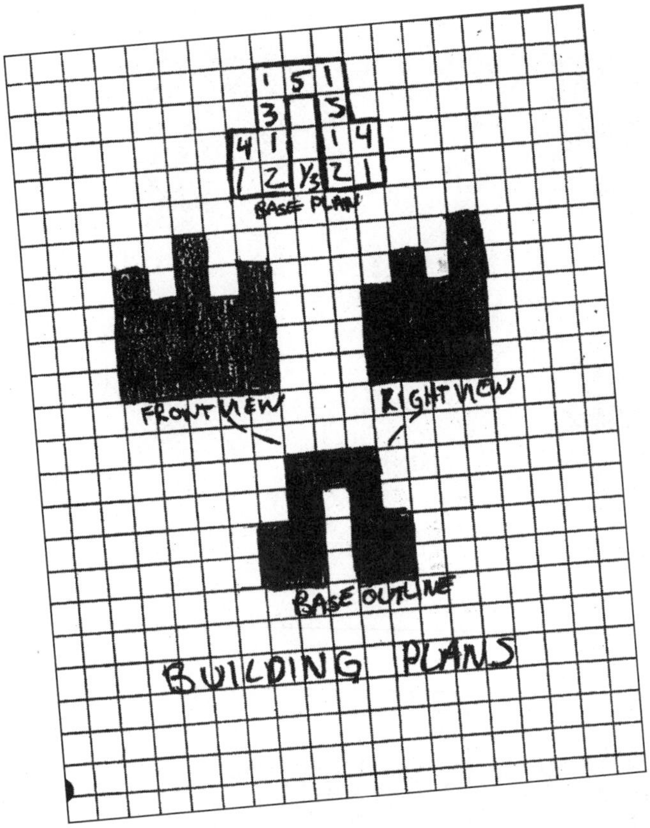
1 5 1
3 5
4 1 1 4
1 2 1/3 2 1
BASE PLAN
FRONT VIEW
RIGHT VIEW
BASE OUTLINE
BUILDING PLANS

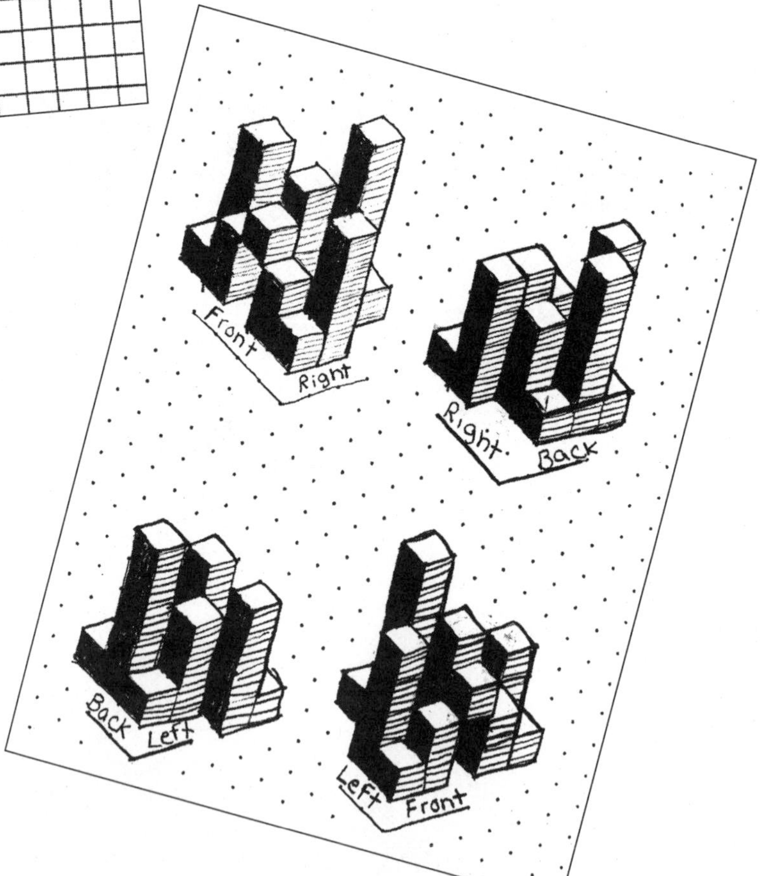
Front
Right
Right
Back
Back
Left
Left
Front

Council of Monterak,
   Our building is an old cathedral. This building could provide great heritage to the people on Montarek.
   This building can attrack tourist to see the old cathedral. Tourism could greatly help boost the economy in Montarek.
   It can provide a good historical marking when Monterak becomes modern. People can worship there and see how Monterak was back then in ancient times. It can show the students of Monterak art masterpieces and the architecture of the building. Our catherdral will provide a lot of education, history, and beatiful sightseeing for the city of Monetrak.

A Teacher's Comments

My students worked in pairs on this project. I gave them one full class period and ten minutes in each of two other class periods to work together. Pairs that needed more time worked outside of class.

Drawings

*Base plan—*2 out of 3 points

The base plan was accurate except where students wrote "1/3." I took off 1 point for this notation. It seems they were trying to show that they had balanced one cube as a type of arch in the "third story." Their notation did not fit the "rules" we had established in the unit; in the unit, we used this notation to indicate that either 1 or 3 cubes could be placed in the given position. To receive credit for this notation, they should have included a note explaining their notation and the fact that the notation strategy used in class was too limiting to show the arch in their building.

*Set of building plans—*6 out of 6 points

All three of the views were drawn accurately.

*Isometric views—*9 out of 12 points

The front right and right back views are accurate. The left front view does not show one of the four-cube towers shown in the base plan. In the back left, the same four-cube tower is drawn as a three-cube tower. The back left view also misses the "arch" cube and one of the two-cube towers from the front of the building. Although there were mistakes in two of the four views, I gave partial credit for these views since many aspects were accurate.

Letter

*Composition—*2 out of 3 points

The letter to the Council of Montarek is convincing and complete. The students described what the building would be used for and gave several reasons for why it would be useful to citizens. I took 1 point off because I was a bit confused when students wrote about constructing an "old" building and when they said that their city is not modern now, but will be someday. These statements do not make sense in the context of the situation.

*Structure—*2 out of 2 points

The report was neat, and the sentences were complete and properly punctuated.

Project Constraints

4 out of 4 points

The students used 30 cubes for their building, and the work is neat and organized.

These students received an overall score of 25 out of 30 points. In my class, that is a B+. They showed a good understanding of the required elements in the report. The errors might have been cleared up if they had checked their work more carefully.

Reflection

Some of the errors in the isometric views might have been caused by cubes falling off the model (for example, a four-cube tower became a three-cube tower). Buildings made from this many cubes are not very stable. Rotating the models to see different corners caused avalanches that required students to reconstruct their buildings. To help with this problem in the future, I will have students pull apart the tables and spread their groups out as much as possible.

To help reduce errors, I am going to suggest that each pair of students have someone else help them edit their reports and drawings. The partners seemed too close to their work to edit it adequately.

I was also concerned and disappointed with my students' project displays. Their work was attractive, but their displays were lacking. I realize that they do not have much experience constructing and organizing displays of their work. Next time I will do some brainstorming with my students about interesting ways to display their projects. I may find that I need to construct sample displays to help them think harder about this aspect of the project.

Blackline Masters

Figures for Problem 1.2

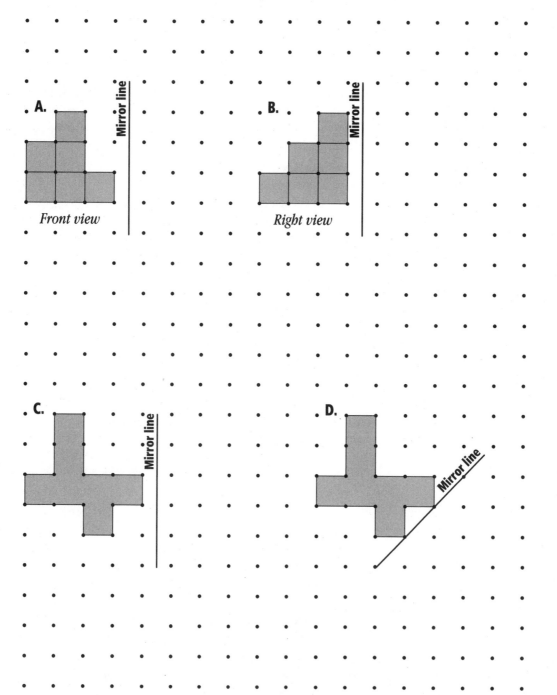

A. **Mirror line**

Front view

B. **Mirror line**

Right view

C. **Mirror line**

D. **Mirror line**

Figures for Problem 1.2 Follow-Up

1a.

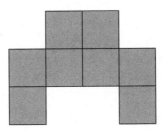

1b.

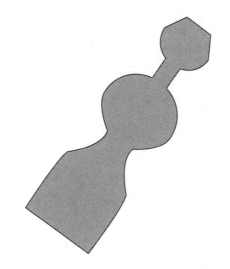

2.

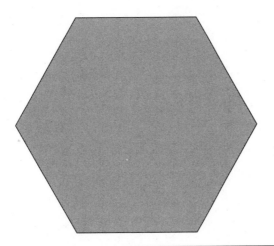

ACE Questions 16 and 17

16.

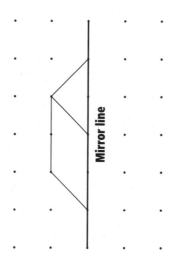

17.

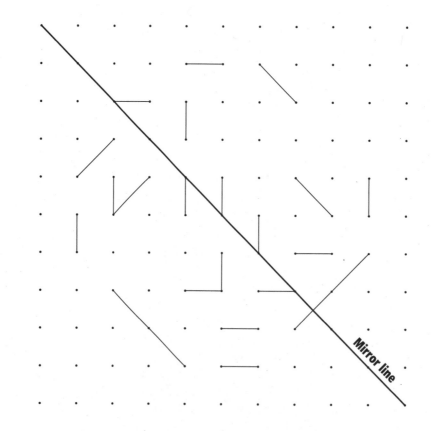

Base Outlines for Problem 3.1

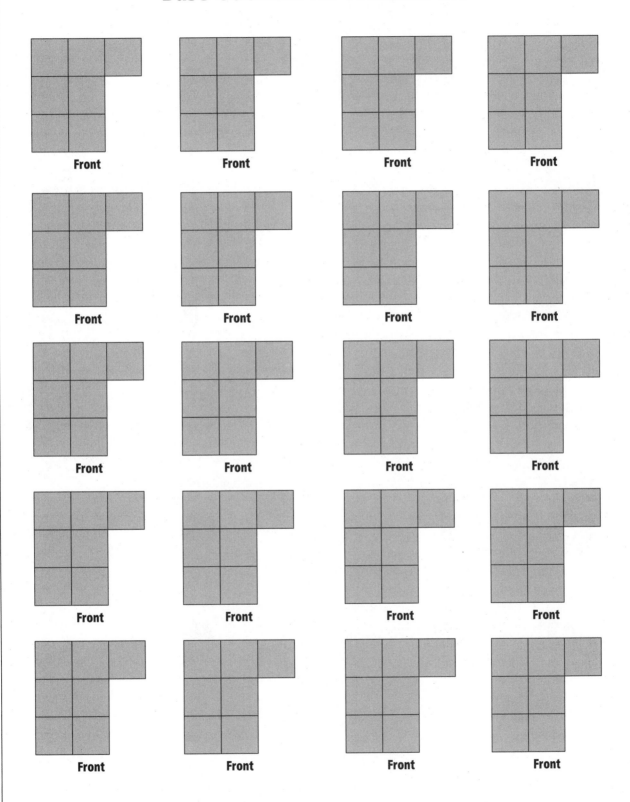

2-D Design Cubes

Corner Views from Problem 6.1

A. Building _____

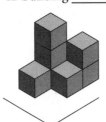

B. Building _____

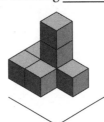

C. Building _____

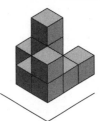

D. Building _____

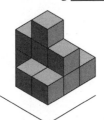

E. Building _____

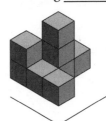

F. Building _____

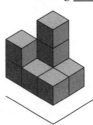

G. Building _____

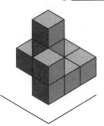

H. Building _____

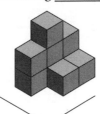

I. Building _____

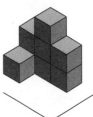

J. Building _____

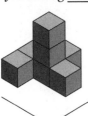

K. Building _____

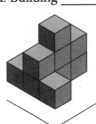

L. Building _____

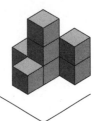

Buildings from Problem 6.4

A.

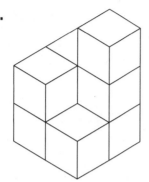

B.

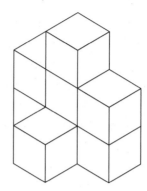

C.

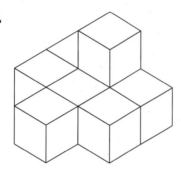

D.

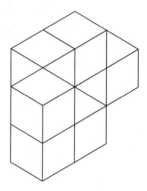

E.

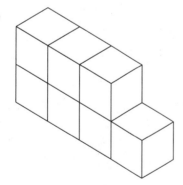

F.

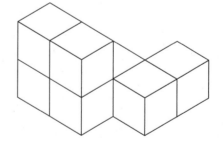

Base outline

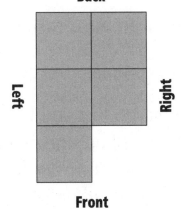

Base plan

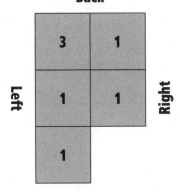

Use the base outline on page 8 to construct the first layer of the building on your building mat.

How many cubes do you need to construct the bottom layer?

Now use the base plan to complete the building.

If you turn the building mat so that you look at the front, back, left, or right of your cube building straight on, you will see a two-dimensional pattern of squares. Turn the building on your mat and decide which side of the building (front, back, left, or right) Emily was looking at when she made these diagrams:

A.

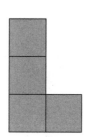

B.

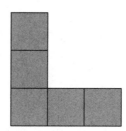

C.

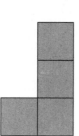

D.

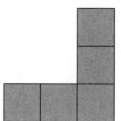

Labsheet 1.2A shows the figures below. For each drawing, set the edge of a mirror on the mirror line so that the reflecting surface is facing the cube diagram. Sketch the mirror image on the other side of the mirror line, and label the image. If the image is the opposite of the *front*, it must be the *back*. If it is the opposite of the *right*, it must be the *left*.

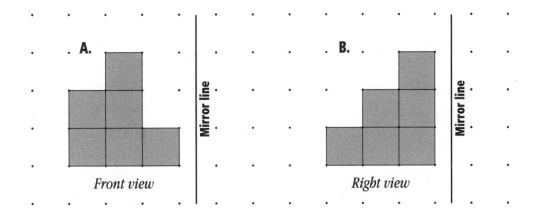

A. *Front view*

B. *Right view*

Labsheet 1.2A also shows the polygons below. Try to imagine what the mirror image of each figure would look like. On the labsheet, draw what you think the image will look like. Use a mirror to check your prediction.

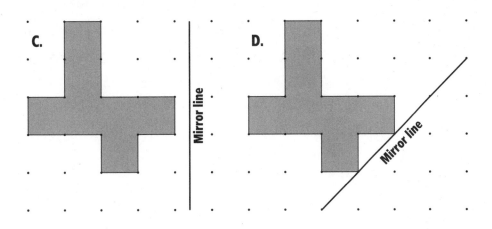

C.

D.

Construct this building on your building mat:

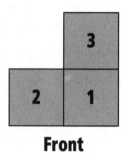

Front

A. Draw the base outline of the building on a piece of grid paper. Remember that the base outline shows the cubes that touch the building mat. Then, draw and label the front, back, left, and right views.

B. Remove a cube from the building. Draw a base outline and a set of views for the new building.

C. Return the cube you removed so that you again have the original building. Now, add three more cubes to the building. Draw a base outline and a set of views for the new building.

Some of the stone fragments show the front and right views of a building from the ancient city of Montarek.

A. The etchings show this front view of the building:

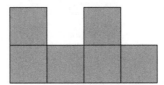

On your grid paper, draw the back view.

B. The etchings show this right view of the building:

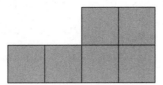

On your grid paper, draw the left view.

C. Use your cubes to build a building that matches your four views.

D. Do you think there is more than one building with the front and right views etched on the tablets and the back and left views you have sketched on grid paper? Explain your answer.

Emily found a fragment of a stone tablet with this base plan etched on it:

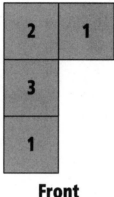

Front

On your building mat, construct the building represented by the base plan.

Emily also found the three sets of building plans shown on the next page on stone tablets. Does one of the three sets of plans correspond to the building you made using the base plan? If so, which one?

Set 1

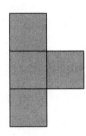

Base outline

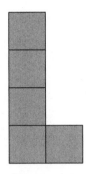

Front view

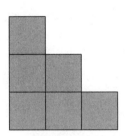

Right view

Set 2

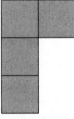

Base outline

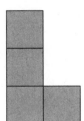

Front view

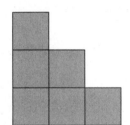

Right view

Set 3

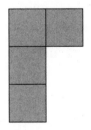

Base outline

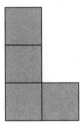

Front view

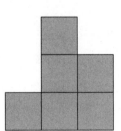

Right view

Below are base plans for four different buildings. With your group, construct a model of each building on a building mat.

A.

2	1	2
2	3	
2	1	

Front

B.

1	1	2
3	1	
2	1	

Front

C.

2	1	1
3	2	
1	1	

Front

D.

1	2	1
2	3	
1	1	

Front

Now, use your observation skills to match your buildings with the drawings on the next page. When you are finished, discuss your ideas with your group and try to reach consensus about which views go with which building.

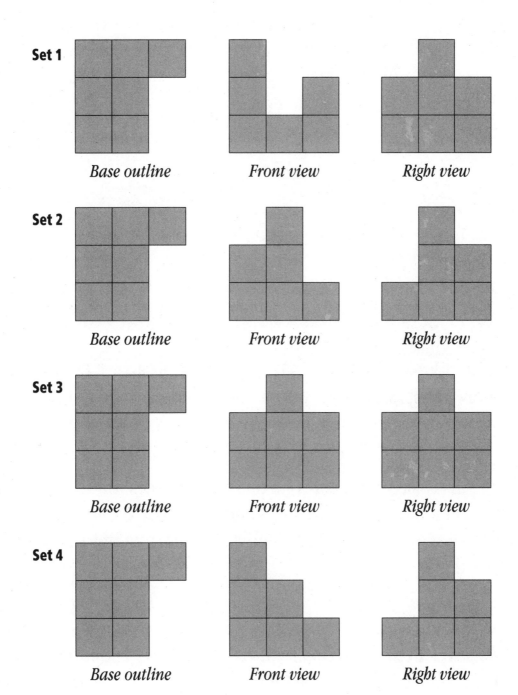

Set 1

Base outline *Front view* *Right view*

Set 2

Base outline *Front view* *Right view*

Set 3

Base outline *Front view* *Right view*

Set 4

Base outline *Front view* *Right view*

In A and B, construct the building represented by the base plan. Then, make a set of building plans for each building on grid paper. Remember that a set of building plans consists of the base outline, the front view, and the right view.

A.

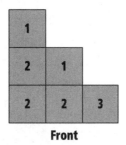

Front

B.

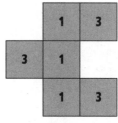

Front

C. Emily has studied some ancient writings she found among the ruins of Montarek. She thinks that one of the two buildings was used as a lookout post to watch for the approach of enemies or friendly travelers. Look at your building plans of the two buildings. Which do you think might have been used as a lookout post? Write at least two or three sentences to explain your answer.

D. Emily has discovered part of a diary kept by one of the residents of ancient Montarek. The diary indicates that the resident lived in the building from part A. Emily shows you a translated entry from the diary:

After dinner I went upstairs to my room. The stars were very bright, so I made my way to the tower from where I gazed at the stars. I can look down on the roof of my room from the tower, but I cannot see the tower from the windows of my room.

By examining your cube model from part A, the building plans you made for the building, and clues from the diary entry, identify which cube(s) on the building might have been the location of the resident's room. Write an explanation for your answer.

Emily Hawkins uncovered six ancient stone tablets in her last expedition to the ruins of Montarek. A set of building plans is drawn on each tablet. The plans are shown below and on the next page. Use cubes to make a model of a building corresponding to each set of plans.

As you make each building, compare your models with those of other students in your class. Note how the other cube models are like yours and how they are different. Record a base plan for each building so that you can share what you did with the class.

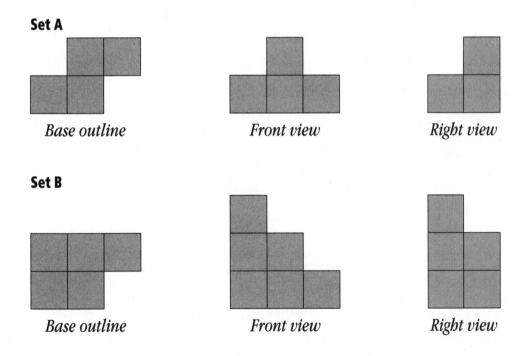

Set A

Base outline   *Front view*   *Right view*

Set B

Base outline   *Front view*   *Right view*

Set C

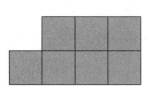

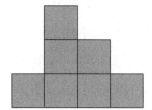 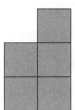

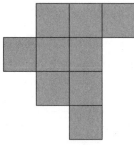

Base outline   *Front view*   *Right view*

Set D

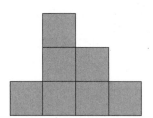 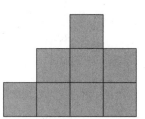

Base outline   *Front view*   *Right view*

Set E

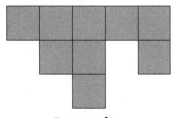 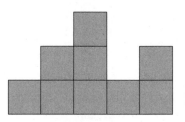 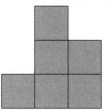

Base outline   *Front view*   *Right view*

Set F

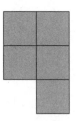 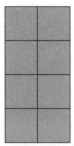 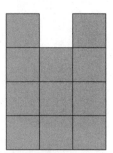

Base outline   *Front view*   *Right view*

An incomplete set of plans is shown in A–C. In each case, one of the three diagrams is missing—either the base outline, the front view, or the right view. On grid paper, draw the missing view and a base plan for each building.

A.

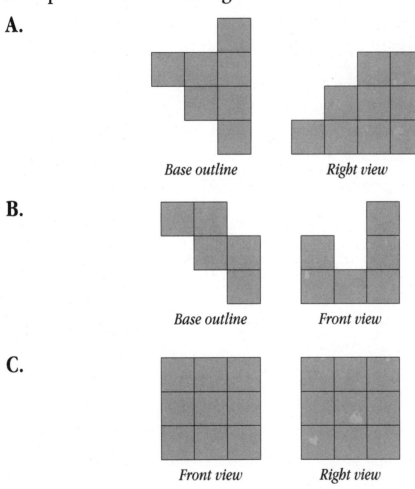

Base outline   *Right view*

B.

Base outline   *Front view*

C.

Front view   *Right view*

D. What is the greatest number of cubes you can use and still fit the plans given in part C? Make a base plan for a building with the greatest number of cubes.

E. What is the least number of cubes you can use and still fit the plans given in part C? Make a base plan for a building with the least number of cubes.

With your cubes, make a building that corresponds to this set of building plans:

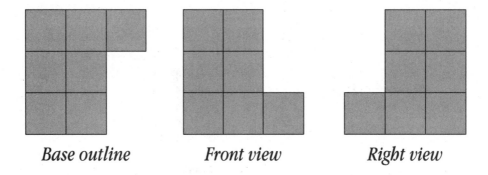

Base outline   *Front view*   *Right view*

A. Draw the base plan of your building. Compare your base plan with the base plans made by other students in your group.

B. How many different buildings can be made from this set of building plans? Work with your group until you are sure you have found all of the different buildings. Draw a base plan for each building.

The plans in A–C were discovered by Emily among the ruins of Montarek. For each set of plans, find a minimal building and the maximal building. Record the base plans for your minimal building and the maximal building on grid paper. For each part, compare your minimal and maximal base plans with those of others in your class or group.

A.

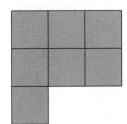
Base outline

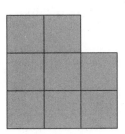
Front view

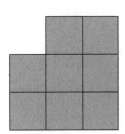
Right view

B.

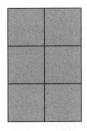
Base outline

Front view

Right view

C.

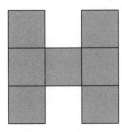
Base outline

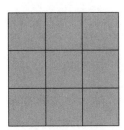
Front view

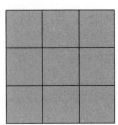
Right view

A. Work with your group to construct a minimal building from the set of building plans. Make a base plan of your building on grid paper.

B. Work with your group to construct the maximal building from the set of building plans. Make a base plan of your building on grid paper.

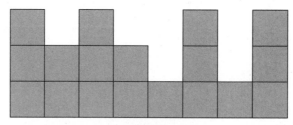

Base outline

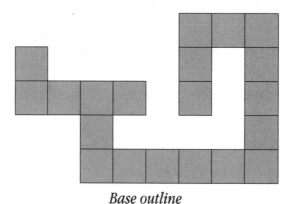

Front view

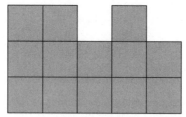

Right view

Hold a cube level with your eyes. Look at the cube carefully. Turn it to see each of its corners. Tip the cube so that you see the corner nearest you in the center with six vertices evenly spaced around this center corner. Your challenge is to find a way to draw the cube in exactly this position on a sheet of isometric dot paper.

When you and your partner have each successfully drawn the cube, try to find a way to show a different view of the cube in a picture on the dot paper. The two pictures should look quite different. One should show the top of the cube and one should show the bottom.

Make a stack using three cubes. Hold the stack in the air and turn it, observing it from many different views.

  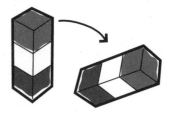

Your challenge is to find every way this stack of three cubes can be pictured on isometric dot paper.

You can use your 2-D cube models to help you draw your pictures. Be sure you stack the models in the same way that the real cubes are stacked. You can place the 2-D models on the dot paper so you can better see where to draw the lines.

Talk to your partner and check each other's work so that you can both get better at drawing models of cube arrangements on isometric dot paper.

A. Use four cubes to make the building shown below. On isometric dot paper, make as many drawings of this cube building, turned in the air in different ways, as you can.

B. Explain why you think you have found all possible ways to draw the building on isometric dot paper.

A. On your building mat, create a building using at least 7 cubes but no more than 12 cubes. Make a drawing of it on isometric dot paper. Label the drawing to indicate which corner the building is being viewed from (front right, right back, back left, or left front).

B. Now turn the building and make a drawing from the opposite corner. Label the view to indicate the corner.

C. If you give a friend just these two drawings, do you think he or she will be able to construct the building exactly as you have made it? Explain.

D. Exchange the isometric dot paper drawings that you made with the drawings that your partner made. Construct a cube building from your partner's drawings.

E. Were you able to get enough information from the drawings to re-create the building your partner constructed? Explain why or why not.

F. Was your partner able to re-create your building from your drawings? Why or why not?

G. In the last investigation, you found that a set of building plans does not always allow you to construct a unique building. However, if you specify that the building must be maximal, it will be unique. Do you think a set of two diagrams on isometric dot paper corresponds to a unique building? Or, is it possible that more than one building can be made from a set of two diagrams on isometric dot paper?

A. Make the base plan for the ziggurat shown below.

B. Working with a partner, build the ziggurat with cubes, and make a set of building plans for it.

C. Why do you suppose people from ancient Montarek would build such pyramids? Explain your thoughts.

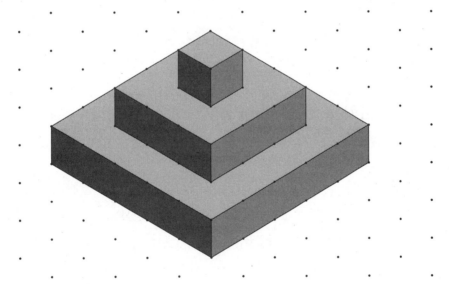

Below are sketches of base plans that Emily Hawkins found in the diary of an architect who was a citizen of ancient Montarek.

1	1	1
1	2	1
1	1	1

Front

3	3	3	3	3
3	5	5	5	3
3	5	6	5	3
3	5	5	5	3
3	3	3	3	3

Front

A. Construct a model of the first ziggurat from cubes. Then, use your model to sketch a set of building plans for the ziggurat on grid paper.

B. Use cubes to construct a model of the second ziggurat. Make a sketch of the ziggurat on isometric dot paper. Look back at the ziggurat from Problem 5.1 if you are unsure of how to begin.

C. Compare the representations you have made of the two ziggurats. Write a short paragraph explaining to Emily which of the three representations—the cube model, the building plans, or the sketch on isometric dot paper—is the most useful for describing a ziggurat.

In your group, build a cube model of each of these buildings on your building mat. Page 73 shows views of each building from all four corners. These views also appear on Labsheet 6.1. Match each model to its corner views. On the labsheet, label each view with the building number and the corner from which the building is being viewed: left front, front right, back left, or right back.

Building 1

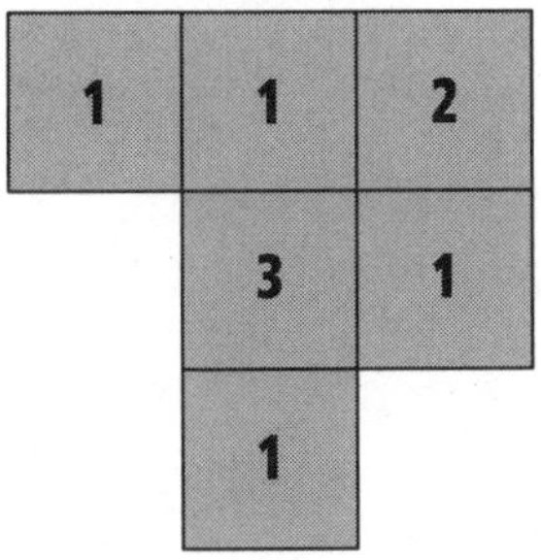

1	1	2
	3	1
	1	

Front

Building 2

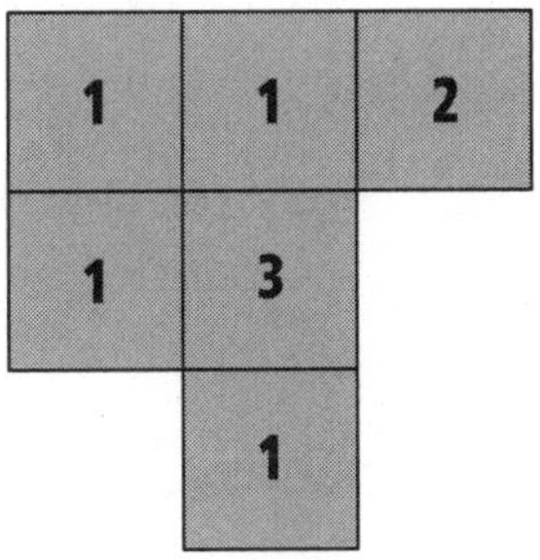

1	1	2
1	3	
	1	

Front

Building 3

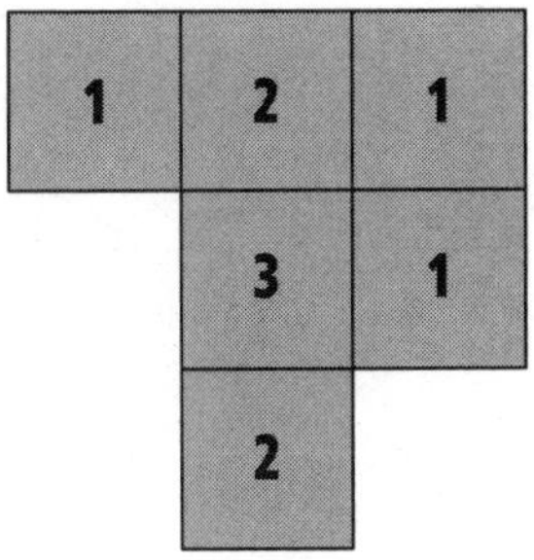

1	2	1
	3	1
	2	

Front

In each drawing, visualize what the figure would look like if the shaded cubes were removed. Make an isometric drawing of the result. If you need to, build the model from cubes and look at it.

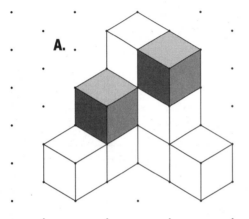

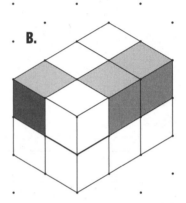

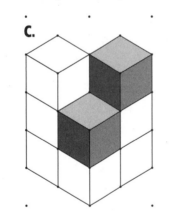

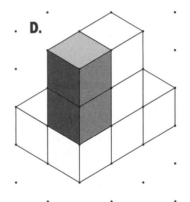

In each drawing, one or more cube faces are shaded. Picture what the model would look like with a cube added to each shaded face. Make an isometric drawing of the result.

A.

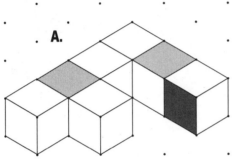

B.

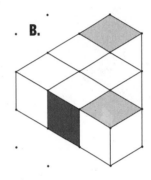

C.

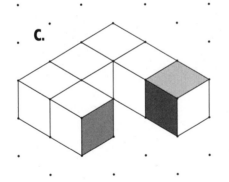

D.

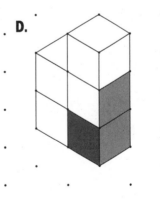

In A–F, experiment with the two basic shapes to make the building shown. Shade the drawings on your labsheet to show how you put the pieces together to make the shape.

A.

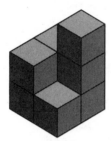

B.

C.

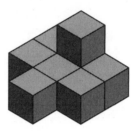

D.

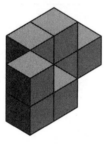

E.

F.

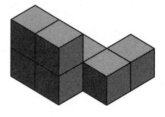

Dear Family,

The next unit in your child's course of study in mathematics class this year is *Ruins of Montarek*. It is designed to develop skills at visualizing and drawing representations of solid figures made from cubes. Such spatial visualization skills are too often neglected in mathematics curriculums.

The investigations in *Ruins of Montarek* center on a character named Emily Hawkins, an explorer and adventurer studying the ruins of an ancient city. Students learn to use the visual clues that Emily finds to construct cube models of ancient buildings. Students also learn to make three different types of drawings for representing cube buildings and examine the strengths and weaknesses of each representation. In particular, students address questions of uniqueness: Does this set of drawings represent only one building, or can I create several different buildings from these drawings? Is there a constraint I can add to these drawings so that they represent only one building?

This unit also addresses the idea of line symmetry. Students are introduced to line symmetry when they use mirrors to reflect figures over a mirror line. They then learn that sometimes you can draw a mirror line, or a line of symmetry, on a figure itself.

You can help your child with his or her work for this unit in several ways:

- Provide sugar cubes or other cubes for your child to use for the homework problems. Many of these problems are much easier if students use cubes to build and experiment.

- Ask your child about what he or she is learning in class. Your child may enjoy teaching you how to make and read the different kinds of building plans studied in class.

- Look over your child's homework and make sure all questions are answered and that explanations are clear.

As always, if you have any questions or concerns about this unit or your child's progress in class, please feel free to call. All of us here are interested in your child and want to be sure that this year's mathematics experiences are enjoyable and promote a firm understanding of mathematics.

Sincerely,

Estimada familia,

La próxima unidad del programa de matemáticas de su hijo o hija para este curso se llama *Ruins of Montarek* (*Las ruinas de Montarek*). La misma ha sido diseñada para perfeccionar las destrezas relacionadas con la visualización y el trazado de representaciones de figuras geométricas hechas con cubos. Muchas veces, a dichas destrezas de visualización espacial no se les da mucha importancia en los programas de matemáticas.

Las investigaciones de esta unidad se centran en un personaje llamado Emily Hawkins, exploradora y aventurera que examina las ruinas de una ciudad de la antigüedad. Los alumnos aprenden a usar las indicaciones visuales que Emily encuentra para construir modelos hechos con cubos de edificios antiguos. Además, se les enseña a hacer tres tipos diferentes de dibujos para representar edificios de cubos y a examinar los aspectos positivos y negativos de cada una de las representaciones. En concreto, los alumnos abordan preguntas relacionadas con la singularidad de los objetos: ¿Representa esta serie de dibujos un solo edificio o puedo crear varios edificios diferentes con los dibujos? ¿Hay alguna restricción que pueda agregar a estos dibujos para que representen un solo edificio?

En esta unidad se trata también la idea de simetría lineal. A los alumnos se les expondrá esta idea cuando utilicen espejos para reflejar figuras sobre una línea especular. Descubrirán que a veces se puede trazar una línea especular, o un eje de simetría, en la propia figura.

Para ayudar a su hijo o hija con el trabajo de esta unidad, ustedes pueden hacer lo siguiente:

- Denle cubos de azúcar u otro tipo de cubos para que los utilice cuando haga los problemas de la tarea. Muchos le resultarán más fáciles si emplea cubos en las construcciones y en los experimentos.

- Pregúntenle acerca de lo que está aprendiendo en clase. Quizás disfrute enseñándoles a hacer y a leer los diferentes tipos de planos de edificios tratados en clase.

- Repasen su tarea para asegurarse de que conteste todas las preguntas y escriba con claridad las explicaciones.

Y como de costumbre, si ustedes necesitan más detalles o aclaraciones respecto a esta unidad o sobre los progresos de su hijo o hija en esta clase, no duden en llamarnos. A todos nos interesa su hijo o hija y queremos asegurarnos de que las experiencias matemáticas que tenga este año sean lo más amenas posibles y ayuden a fomentar en él o ella una sólida comprensión de las matemáticas.

Atentamente,

Additional Practice

Investigations

Answer Key

Investigation 1

1. For each of the base plans below, make a set of building plans for the building on grid paper. Remember that a set of building plans includes a base outline, the front view, and the right view of the building.

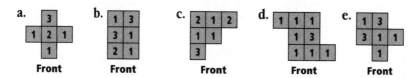

2. For each of the base plans below, make a cube model of the building and then match the building to the correct set of building plans.

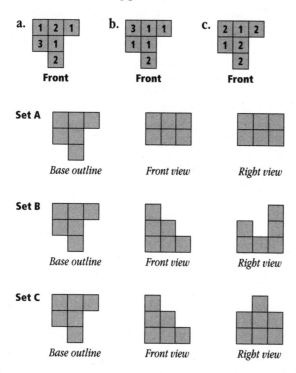

3. Emily Hawkins has found a description of a building that once stood in the city of Montarek. Emily would like to make a cube model of the building, but all she can tell from the description is that five cubes are needed for the model and that the base outline looks like this:

Front

a. Using five cubes, make a building that fits the conditions described. Record the base plan of your building.

b. Is there more than one building that meets the conditions described? If no other building is possible, explain why. If other buildings are possible, provide a base plan for each one.

Investigation 2

1. Using your cubes, make a model of the building shown in this base plan:

Front

   a. Sketch a set of building plans for the building on grid paper. Remember that a set of building plans includes the base outline, the front view, and the right view.

   b. Add as many cubes as you can to the building to make a different building that has the same set of building plans. Make a base plan for your new building.

   c. Explain how your new building can have the same set of building plans as the original building even though your new building has a different base plan.

2. Record a base plan for the building with the following set of building plans.

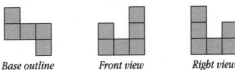

   Base outline   *Front view*   *Right view*

3. Use your cubes to make the building shown in this base plan:

Front

   a. Sketch a set of building plans for the building on grid paper.

   b. What is the greatest number of cubes you can add to the building to create a new building with the same set of building plans as the original building? Explain your answer and sketch a base plan of the new building.

4. Below are the base outline and right view of a building:

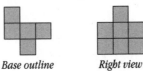

   Base outline   *Right view*

   Of the three front views below, which one is *not* a possible front view for a building with the above base outline and right view? Explain your reasoning.

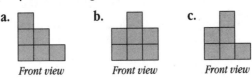

   a.   b.   c.

   Front view   *Front view*   *Front view*

Investigation 3

1. Use the set of building plans below for parts a, b, and c.

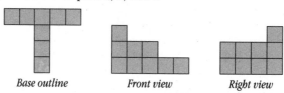

Base outline *Front view* *Right view*

   a. Use your cubes to make a minimal building from the above building plans. Sketch a base plan of the building on grid paper.

   b. Use your cubes to make a maximal building from the above building plans. Sketch a base plan of the building on grid paper.

   c. How many more cubes are needed to make the maximal building than a minimal building?

2. Emily Hawkins found the incomplete set of building plans below among the ruins of Montarek:

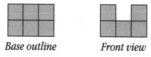

Base outline *Front view*

   a. She also found that ten cubes are needed to make the model for the building. Use ten cubes to make a model that fits the above plans, and make a base plan for your building on grid paper.

   b. On grid paper, sketch the right view of your building.

   c. Do you think that the building you constructed in part a is the only building with 10 cubes that fits the incomplete plans? Explain your reasoning.

   d. Make a building that fits the incomplete plans and that has the fewest cubes possible. Make a base plan of your building on grid paper.

3. Jennifer has sketched this set of building plans on grid paper:

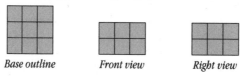

Base outline *Front view* *Right view*

   a. Jennifer claims that she can make a building that fits the above plans using 12 cubes. Use 12 cubes to make a building that matches the above plans. Sketch a base plan of your building on grid paper.

   b. Do you think your building is the same building Jennifer made? Explain your reasoning.

   c. What is the greatest number of cubes you can add to your building so that the new building has the same building plans? Sketch a base plan for this new building on grid paper.

   d. Is there another building that fits Jennifer's building plans and has the same number of cubes you used for your building in part c? Explain your reasoning.

Investigation 4

1. Copy each of the buildings below, exactly as it appears, on isometric dot paper. One cube in each building is shaded so you can tell how many cubes to use.

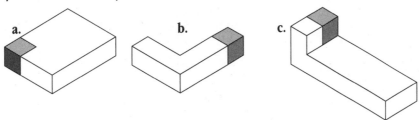

2. For each of the buildings shown below, make a sketch on isometric dot paper showing what the building would look like if the shaded cubes were removed.

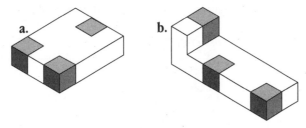

3. Use the sketch of the building shown below for parts a, b, and c.

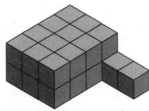

   a. On a piece of grid paper, sketch a set of building plans for the building. Remember that a set of building plans includes the base outline, the front view, and the right view.

   b. Is the building a maximal building, a minimal building, or neither? Explain your reasoning.

   c. How many cubes would you need to make a model of the building? Explain how you found your answer.

Investigation 5

1. Below is a base plan for a building that Emily Hawkins has discovered. Use the base plan to answer the following questions.

2	2	2	2	2
2	1	1	1	2
2	1		1	2
2	1	1	1	2
2	2	2	2	2

Front

   a. Use your cubes to make a model of this building. Sketch a set of building plans for the building, including the base outline, the front view, and the right view.

   b. Is this building a maximal building, a minimal building, or neither? Explain your reasoning.

   c. Emily says that this kind of building was called an "inverted ziggurat" by the people of ancient Montarek. Write two or three sentences explaining why this kind of building might be called an inverted ziggurat.

2. Use the sketch of the ziggurat below to answer the following questions.

   a. The above view is from the front right corner. On isometric dot paper, sketch what the ziggurat would look like from the front left corner.

   b. Does your sketch look any different than the sketch from the front-right corner? Why or why not?

Investigation 6

1. Visualize what this model would look like with the shaded cubes removed. Draw an isometric view of the resulting model from this same corner.

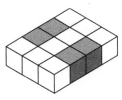

2. The building below is drawn from the front right corner. Draw an isometric view of the building from the back left corner.

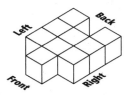

3. Visualize what this model would look like if cubes were added to the shaded faces. Draw an isometric view of the resulting model from this same corner.

Answer Keys

Investigation 1

1. a.

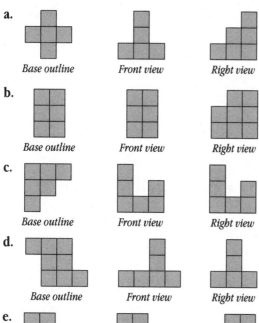

Base outline   Front view   Right view

b.

Base outline   Front view   Right view

c.

Base outline   Front view   Right view

d.

Base outline   Front view   Right view

e.

Base outline   Front view   Right view

2. a. Set C   **b.** Set B   **c.** Set A

3. a. Possible answer:

b. There are six possible buildings because after using three cubes to form the base outline, the remaining two cubes can be placed in a total of six different ways to form six different buildings.

Investigation 2

1. a.

Base outline   Front view   Right view

b.

c. While adding more cubes changes the building, it may not change the front or right views because cubes can be added in back or to the left of existing cubes so they are "hidden" from the front and right views.

2.

3. a.

Base outline   Front view   Right view

b. Two additional cubes can be added to the building without changing the building plans. The base plan for the new building will be exactly the same as the original except that two cubes are stacked on every square of the base outline. The two additional cubes change the building but do not alter the two-dimensional front or right views (i.e., the additional cubes change the building in term of "depth" but not in terms of "length" and "width").

4. Front view b is not possible because the stack of three cubes cannot be placed so the front view and right view are the same (and if b were possible, then the front and right views would be the same).

Investigation 3

1. a.   b. | 3 | 2 | ② | 1 | 1 |

c. Only one cube can be added to the minimal building to make the maximal building.

2. a. | 2 | 1 | 2 |
       | 2 | 1 | 2 | b.

c. The building is unique because it is a maximal building.

d. Possible answer: | 2 | 1 | 1 |
                     | 1 | 1 | 2 | A minimal building can be made that fits the incomplete plans using eight cubes (multiple buildings are possible).

3. a. Possible answer: | 1 | 1 | 2 |
                       | 1 | 2 | 1 |
                       | 2 | 1 | 1 |
                          Front

b. The building made in a is not necessarily the same building Jennifer made because it is a minimal building and therefore is not unique.

c.   Six cubes can be added to Jennifer's building without changing the building plans.

2	2	2
2	2	2
2	2	2
Front

d. No; The building made in part c is unique because it is a maximal building.

Investigation 4

1. **a.–c.** Check students' work for accuracy. Be sure they sketch the entire shape (including the shaded part of each figure).

2. **a.–b.** Check students' work for accuracy. Be sure they have drawn the figures without the shaded cubes. The shading of the cubes to be removed in the figures should make it relatively easy for the students to visualize what their final shape should look like, but they may need help connecting the correct segments on their dot paper to get the correct perspective.

    Students' final sketches should look like this:

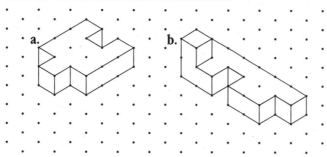

3. **a.**

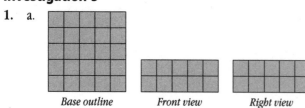

       Base outline   *Front view*   *Right view*

  b. The building is a maximal building since no cubes can be added without changing the set of building plans.

  c. Counting the cubes from the drawing, 26 cubes would be needed to make a model of the building.

Investigation 5

1. **a.**

       Base outline   *Front view*   *Right view*

  b. The building is a minimal building. No cubes can be removed without changing the building plans, but more cubes can be added to the building without changing the building plans.

  c. Answers will vary. Note that the empty space inside the building looks like a small ziggurat turned upside down (i.e., a 3×3 layer of base cubes for the base outline and one cube stacked on the center cube.)

2. a.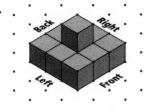

b. The ziggurat looks the same from every corner because it is symmetric about its center.

Investigation 6

1.

2.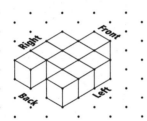

3.

base plan A drawing of the base outline of a building with a number in each square indicating the number of cubes in the stack at that position.

building mat A sheet of paper used for drawing a set of building plans. You use a mat labeled "Front," "Back," "Left," and "Right" in order to position cubes correctly.

isometric dot paper Dot paper in which the distances from a dot to each of the six surrounding dots are all equivalent. The word *isometric* comes from the Greek words *iso*, which means "same," and *metric*, which means "measure."

line of symmetry A line through a figure so that if the figure were folded on the line, the two parts of the figure would match up exactly.

maximal building The building satisfying a given set of building plans and having the greatest possible number of cubes. The maximal building for a set of plans is unique.

minimal building A building satisfying a given set of plans and having the least possible number of cubes. The minimal building for a set of plans is not necessarily unique.

set of building plans A set of three diagrams—the front view, the right view, and the base outline.

unique One of a kind. When we say that the building corresponding to a set of plans is unique, we mean that it is the only building that matches the plans.

ziggurat A pyramid-shaped building made up of layers in which each layer is a square smaller than the square beneath it.

Index

Index

constructing from two-dimensional representations, 25n, 26–32, 39a–39d, 39h, 40–44, 51a–51d

cube buildings, 6b, 7–18, 25a–25h

matching with an isometric view, 71f, 72–76, 81a–81e

maximal, 39h, 41–44, 51b–51d

minimal, 39h, 41–44, 51b–51d

of a ziggurat, 61l, 62–64, 71a–71c

Mohenjo-Daro, ruins, 26

Original Rebus technique, 61, 81
Orthogonal view, 25b
Overview, 1a–1c

Pacing Chart, 1h
Pattern, ziggurat layer, 63, 71a–71b
Problem-solving goals, 1e

Building Plans, 6b

Describing Unique Buildings, 39h

Isometric Dot Paper Representations, 51h

Making Buildings, 25n

Seeing the Isometric View, 71f

Ziggurats, 61l

Propylaea and the Temple of Athena, 35

Rebus Scenario technique, 26
Rectangular dot paper, 151
Reflection, 6b, 10–12, 25b–25d

ACE, 23–24

Ruins

Machu-Picchu, Peru, 68

Mohenjo-Daro, 26

Propylaea and the Temple of Athena, 35

Spatial skills, 2–5
Spatial visualization

ACE, 77–80

isometric drawing, 1a–1c, 51h, 52–57, 61a–61i, 61l, 62–64, 71a–71c

reading an isometric drawing, 61l, 62–64, 71a–71c, 71f, 72–76, 81a–81e

three-dimensional models from two-dimensional representations, 26–32, 39a–39d, 40–44, 51a–51d

two-dimensional representations, 1a–1c, 6b, 7–18, 25a–25h

Symmetry, 6b, 10–12, 25b–25d

ACE, 23–24, 48

Tchoga Zanbil ziggurat, 63
Technology, 1g
Three-dimensional model

ACE, 19–24, 33–38, 45–50, 65–70, 77–80

constructed from a two-dimensional representation, 25n, 26–32, 39a–39d, 39h, 40–44, 51a–51d

from an isometric representation, 61l, 62–64, 71a–71c

isometric representation of, 51h, 52–57, 61a–61i

matching with an isometric view, 71f, 72–76, 81a–81e

two-dimensional representation of, 2–5, 6b, 7–18, 25a–25h

Transformation, reflection, 6b, 10–12, 23–24, 25b–25d
Transparencies, 117–142
Two-dimensional representation

ACE, 19–24, 33–38, 45–50, 77–80

building plans, 6b, 7–18, 25a–25h

constructing a model from, 25n, 26–32, 39a–39d, 39h, 40–44, 51a–51d

isometric drawing, 1a–1c, 51h, 52–57, 61a–61i

of three-dimensional objects, 1a–1c, 2–5, 6b, 7–18, 25a–25h

reading isometric drawings, 71f, 72–76, 81a–81e

Unique, 41, 147
Unit Project, 1j, 82

assessment guide, 106–111

samples, 107–111

scoring rubric, 106

Vocabulary, 1h
Volume

of an irregular figure, 70

of a cube, 70

Ziggurat, 61l, 62–64, 71a–71c

ACE, 65–70